**New York University**
**CENTER FOR INTERNATIONAL STUDIES**

*Studies in Peaceful Change*

**WHY FEDERATIONS FAIL: An Inquiry into the Requisites for Successful Federalism**
Thomas M. Franck, Gisbert H. Franz, Herbert J. Spiro, and Frank N. Trager.
New York: New York University Press, 1968

**A FREE TRADE ASSOCIATION**
Thomas M. Franck and Edward Weisband.
New York: New York University Press, 1968

**LAW, REASON AND JUSTICE: Essays in Legal Philosophy**
Graham B. Hughes.
New York: New York University Press, Spring 1969

**CZECHOSLOVAKIA: Intervention and Impact**
I. William Zartman.
New York: New York University Press, 1970

**INTERNATIONAL BUSINESS NEGOTIATIONS: A Study in India**
Ashok Kapoor.
New York: New York University Press, 1970

**SIERRA LEONE: Experiment in Democracy in an African Nation**
Gershon Collier.
New York: New York University Press, 1970

**COMPARATIVE CONSTITUTIONAL PROCESS**
Thomas M. Franck.
New York: Frederick A. Praeger, Inc., 1968.

**THE STRUCTURE OF IMPARTIALITY**
Thomas M. Franck.
New York: The Macmillan Company, 1968

**AGENTS OF CHANGE: A Close Look at the Peace Corps**
David Hapgood and Meridan Bennett.
Boston: Little, Brown and Company, 1968

# Sierra Leone

## Studies in Peaceful Change

Prepared Under the Auspices of
The Center for International Studies, New York University.

New York: New York University Press
London: University of London Press Ltd
1970

# Sierra Leone

## Experiment in Democracy in an African Nation

*by Gershon Collier*

*To* FASHU, *my wife, whose selfless love and unflagging devotion have been constant sources of inspiration in my life.*

# Preface

African contemporary history and politics have recently achieved a new significance particularly in the curricula of many universities and schools all over the world. This development has been especially true of the United States where the struggles for racial equality and a growing awareness of the inevitability of a universal black identity have brought a new dimension to the problems related to the black experience and a deeper understanding of the history, culture and political problems of Africa.

Too often in the past, African problems have been examined and presented by persons who are not Africans and whose personal knowledge and experience at close range of the African scene have been extremely limited. While there is undoubtably a certain value in such objective interpretation of events, it cannot be denied that in the atmosphere of our times, permeated as it has been by colonialism, imperialism and racism, the subjective approach has a special value if only to provide another perspective of these events.

I wish to record my great indebtedness to the Center for International Studies, New York University, for providing the facilities and the circumstances which gave me the opportunity to embark on this project. I owe a particular debt of gratitude to my mentor and friend, Professor Thomas M. Franck, Professor of Law, New York University, and Director of the Center for International Studies, for his inspiration, encouragement and invaluable friendship without which this book would not have been possible. He not only sponsored the award of the Senior Fellowship which enabled me to spend nearly two rewarding years at the Center for International Studies, New York University, but he also in his inimitable style counselled and guided my efforts

ix

through every stage of my research and writing at a time when I particularly needed his special type of understanding and friendship. He has graciously written the Foreword to this book, for which I also thank him.

I wish to record my appreciation for the colloquia in the Peaceful Change Series at the Center for International Studies where I was able to exchange ideas and receive valuable comments from colleagues. I particularly wish to thank Professor I. William Zartman, Professor of Politics and now Chairman of the Politics Department at New York University and Mr. David Hapgood, formerly of the Peace Corps, then Senior Fellow with me at the Center for International Studies, who read the book in manuscript and gave me valuable encouragement and advice. I wish to thank Miss Joan Jablow who worked with me as a Junior Fellow and gave me useful help in the preparation of the research and material for this book. My special thanks are also due to Miss Alice Bernard-Jones, Assistant Legal Officer of the Legal Department of the United Nations, for the particularly valuable help she gave me with research material as well as exchanging ideas with me on the substance of this book which, as a Sierra Leonean, she was particularly qualified to give.

Let me also express my deep appreciation to Professor Alba Amoia, Professor of Romance Languages at Hunter College and also of the Council on Foreign Relations, who read the book in manuscript and gave invaluable advice, editorial suggestions, and friendly encouragement at all stages of my work.

Finally, I wish to record my indebtedness to Miss Olive Williams, a Sierra Leonean who is a member of the faculty of the Department of Business, Essex County College, New Jersey, for her friendly criticisms and suggestions and for the many hours she gave of her busy schedule to type my changing manuscript many times with understanding and good humour.

G.C.

New York University
New York

# Foreword

It is rare that historical events are recorded by politicians at the once-removed vantage of an academic setting. Also too rare is African contemporary history recorded by African Africanists.

Gershon Collier has incorporated a remarkable range of roles in decolonized Africa: barrister, ambassador, minister, chief justice, and scholar. He has now begun a new career as professor. To some degree, he has always been an observer of the events in which he has participated and a participant in the events he has observed.

To academic purists, this admixture of roles creates the danger of policy-bias. More recently, however, a new generation of academics has accepted the proposition that all research, even in its choice of subject-matter, as well as in its methodology, incorporates elements of subjectivity. Only when these are disguised behind a screen of scientific or metaphysical objectivity do these biases become socially pernicious. When, on the other hand, they are openly stated by the researcher they frequently make for studies that are imbued with red blooded social involvement in the real world. Studies in Peaceful Change must be open to this methodological prescription.

Ambassador Collier's biases are on public record: his passionate anticolonialism and suspicions of neocolonialism, his interest in and sympathetic contacts with the Black movements in the United States, his political support of Prime Minister Albert Margai, even when the latter was advocating a one-party state.

The scholar reading this book may agree or disagree with the social commitments that mark the path of Gershon Collier's career. It is enough that he be aware of them and that he be given an opportunity to observe the contemporary cataclysmic events in Africa through the eyes of a man who has done more than most scholars to shape events and more than most political leaders to try to observe events in social and historical perspective.

Professor Thomas M. Franck,
  Director
New York University
Center for International Studies
New York, New York

# Contents

# Introduction

Sierra Leone had established strong contacts with the outside world nearly five centuries before it achieved independence on April 27, 1961. Yet, with an area of 28,000 square miles and a population of two and a half millions, it remains one of Africa's smallest countries both in size and in population.

Its geographical position on the bulge of the west coast of Africa, from 7° to 10° north latitude and 10° to 13° west longitude, and its possession of excellent watering places and a fine natural harbor have long recommended it as a regular stopping place for ships plying down the coast. This was particularly true during the heyday of Portuguese maritime adventure and exploration. In fact, it is to a fifteenth-century Portuguese explorer that credit has been given for the discovery and naming of the country.

Sierra Leone has one of the heaviest rainfalls in Africa, averaging 115 inches annually. Consequently, its vegetation is dense and the country is replete with tropical forests. It is also mineral rich with large deposits of diamonds and iron ore as well as smaller deposits of bauxite and other minerals. Agriculture, however, dominates the economy; over 70 percent of the people are engaged in it.

Sierra Leone is one of the most beautiful and enchanting countries in the world. The view from the sea with its background of mountains presents a breath-taking and unforgettable spectacle. The mountains were described by an eighteenth-century traveler as rising "gradually from the sea to a stupendous height, richly wooded and

beautifully ornamented by the hand of nature with a variety of delight-
ful prospects." [1] It is to the mountain range, according to one theory,
that the country owes the name *Sierra Leone,* a corruption of the
Portuguese words for "mountains like lions." According to another
theory, the first explorers might have mistaken the sound of the
thunder of a West African storm for the roaring of lions and named
the country for this reason. Whatever the origin may have been, the
name survived in its present resonant and romantic form through the
precolonial and colonial years and was kept at independence.

Although in many ways Sierra Leone may be considered unique
in sub-Sahara Africa, in other ways it has much in common with the
rest of the area. Like many African countries, its early contacts with
Europeans were mainly for trade purposes. When in the sixteenth
century and afterwards the slave trade became the focal point of
European interests in Africa, Sierra Leone knew its human sufferings,
humiliations, and tragedies. It has many tribes, at least thirteen of
which are major ones. There has been incessant intertribal warfare and
often these major tribes have survived at the expense of weaker ones.

Some aspects of traditional life have persisted through the centuries in Sierra Leone, yet numerous influences from the outside have
also left their mark on the lives of the people. From the coast have
come Christianity and Western civilization which, largely through
education and colonialism, have deeply affected and changed the way
of life of the tribes. From the northern Sahara desert routes, Moham-
medanism and Islamic culture have permeated the customs and culture
of Sierra Leone. Because of the sometimes conflicting influences of
these two great religions and cultures, Sierra Leone today is a non-
homogeneous society.

Again like many other African countries, Sierra Leone is peopled
principally by blacks of the negroid stock with only a handful of Europeans, Asians, and Americans who are there almost exclusively for
trade and business purposes. A small but noticeable community of
Lebanese traders has settled in the country and some have intermar-
ried with Sierra Leoneans. But Sierra Leone is unique among African
countries in its history of the early settlement of the Creoles, an
important section of the population. This settlement has left its mark
on the course of events in the nation's history.

In the aftermath of a new appraisal of the problem of slavery
which later led to the complete abolition of this infamous trade,

it was decided to found a home in Africa for freed slaves. Thus the name *Freetown* was given to the settlement in Sierra Leone that came into being toward the end of the eighteenth century through the direct efforts of British philanthropists led by a man named Granville Sharp. Because of the circumstances of the establishment of this settlement, the founding fathers—and later the British Government—did much during the early years of its existence as a colony to make Sierra Leone a model and a convenient home for Africans in Africa. Sierra Leone therefore had a start in educational opportunities and development generally lacking in other African countries. From its University College and secondary schools, doctors, lawyers, missionaries, teachers, traders, and civil servants went out to other parts of Africa to lay the foundations for nation building. British colonial administration in West Africa owed much to the services of Sierra Leoneans who contributed vitally to the smooth operation of the machinery of government. The responsiveness of Sierra Leoneans to Western cultural exposure has been due largely to the influence of the Creole element in the population. The Creoles with their prior contacts with Western education and culture were able effectively to influence the rest of the country, and thus make Sierra Leone unique among African countries.

Before the arrival of Europeans in the country around the fifteenth century, a semblance of democracy prevailed in Sierra Leone through chieftaincy and traditional customary life. The people knew how to wield power. Their kings, chiefs, and rulers at various levels were kept in power by the consent of the people. Since the institutional arrangements were restricted to small tribal communities, the experiences of organized central government were limited. After the British arrived, government in the country became more organized and was increasingly controlled from Britain. In due course, Sierra Leoneans played an ever-increasing role in their government which finally led to independence on April 27, 1961.

The constitution and institutions of government that the British bequeathed Sierra Leone at independence were based on Western ideas of democratic government. Even though some effort was made to recognize the existence of tribal institutions and to use these institutions within the framework of the constitutional system, the real essence of government in Sierra Leone has continued to be democratic in the Western sense.

Since Sierra Leoneans had been adequately prepared—or so the

British thought—by over a century of colonialism, and since the quality of its peoples was exceptional, hopes by the British and the Sierra Leoneans themselves for a successful experiment with democracy were extremely high at the beginning of independence. Furthermore, Sierra Leone had not been the scene of any violent nationalist uprisings against colonialism, nor had its leaders displayed much antagonism against the colonizers. In fact, Sierra Leone was well known for its extremely pro-British sympathies and the great admiration of its peoples for things British and things Western. Enjoying the highest level of education of any country in sub-Sahara Africa, Sierra Leone had a well-trained and experienced indigenous civil service as well as an efficient professional class, including a most efficient Africanized judiciary. The progress of Africanization of the civil service started in the decade before independence, and had almost been completed by 1961. All the omens seemed to indicate that Sierra Leone would succeed after independence and that it might serve as an example for the rest of Africa.

During the first few years of independence, Sierra Leone indeed justified all the high expectations of its admirers and the people themselves felt confident that the forces for progress and the foundations of constitutional democratic government were secure. However, in spite of its history, its experience, its people, and its promise, democracy and constitutional government broke down in Sierra Leone on March 23, 1967—less than six years after the country achieved independence. In the wake of similar events all over Africa, including those in the sister countries of Ghana and Nigeria, the military staged a *coup d'état* and overthrew a popularly elected constitutional government.

The experience of a breakdown and a military takeover has been all too familiar in the recent history of Africa. Most of the African governments achieving independence in the atmospshere of hope of the nineteen-sixties have collapsed in the avalanche of military coups which have swept through the continent. In less than a decade after many independent African nations appeared on the international scene, serious questions are being asked inside and outside of Africa as to the chances of the survival of democracy and stable government on that continent.

The military interveners in Africa have been assuming the role of protectors of the national integrity when they believe the interests of the people to be at stake. By some interesting reasoning, they justify their conduct through stretching the interpretation of their duties as defenders of the security of the state against outside aggression to include responsibility for the defense of the state against internal mismanagement by politicians. Since these military officers are hardly prepared by training and education to administer the government, they have habitually enlisted the alliance of civil servants who themselves may have been implicated in the malpractices and may also have been active collaborators in the corruptions the military pretend to be anxious to correct. The most obvious reason, however, for the military to become the agents of change upon the breakdown of the democratic process in country after country in Africa has been that they constitute the only organized group with the necessary discipline and, through the help of the civil service, the capability to effect these changes. The civil service constitutes the backbone of efficiency and continuity without which immediate collapse and complete chaos would quickly follow the overthrow of constitutional and democratic governments in these African countries.

It is significant that all these countries have had a fairly similar experience and background in colonialism. They inherited upon achieving independence many colossal problems which continued to plague them and to defy solution long after that event. Undoubtedly, political and economic stability after independence have been immeasurably more difficult to achieve because of the particular nature of colonialism and its operation in Africa.

Most of the problems that have bedeviled independence and in many cases have led to the breakdown of the democratic process in African countries have been present in Sierra Leone. They include tribalism, chieftaincy, economic mismanagement, and unsuitable constitutional framework and governmental institutions. In addition, Sierra Leone has been afflicted with the special problems relating to its peculiar Colony-Protectorate status which have made this country's experience unique.

The peoples of Sierra Leone, like those of most African countries, prefer to choose their own leaders and they found it completely intolerable that through the military takeover of 1967 a group of ill-prepared, abrasive officers thirsty for power should have imposed arbitrary rule on them. Though many may have been happy to see the end of a particular group's incumbency, the nation understood and appreciated the system of constitutional government in spite of all the alleged evils and corruptions of the politicians. Thus the more urgent questions confronting countries like Sierra Leone have to do with the establishment and preservation of a stable form of government that will be invulnerable to military or other arbitrary takeovers.

These questions relate directly to the application of democracy to the postcolonial situation. Military and arbitrary rule by themselves have proved quite unsatisfactory and incapable of providing any lasting solutions to the outstanding difficulties existing in Sierra Leone. The army and the civil service comprise men drawn from the same tribal background and conditioned by the same influences as the politicians; not surprisingly, they are afflicted by the same inhibitions that affect the politicians. The main difference, however, apart from the superior experience and education of the latter group, is that the politicians are chosen by the people themselves.

Whatever justification such military groups might have had for seizing power in the first place has tended to disappear progressively the longer they remained in office. For Sierra Leone, with its many years of education and familiarity with democracy, it was particularly agonizing to be governed by a junta of ill-equipped police and army officers. It was therefore not surprising that on April 18, 1968, only a year after the military seized power, a group of young noncommissioned officers staged a counter coup against their own superiors, charged them with corruption, and threw out the military regime. They established what they called the Anti-Corruption Revolutionary Movement. One week later, in keeping with a promise they had made, they installed a civilian government with Siaka Stevens, the leader of the All People's Congress, as Prime Minister.

Thus once again Sierra Leone established a favorable record in the unhappy story of independence in postcolonial Africa. Of the three [2] former British Colonial territories in West Africa to be afflicted by military takeovers, Sierra Leone was the first to be returned to civilian rule. How successfully the country will survive these experiences is another matter altogether.

However, since the experience of democracy in postcolonial Sierra Leone has been on the whole so similar to that elsewhere, a study of the Sierra Leone experiment should prove illuminating for the understanding of contributory factors in the breakdown of democracy in other postcolonial African nations as well as the understanding of other broad problems of democracy in Africa.

It was my privilege to participate actively in the politics of Sierra Leone immediately prior to the granting of independence. Through my activities as an executive member and one of the founding leaders of the People's National Party, and also through my frequent appearances in the courts of Sierra Leone during that period as a lawyer in the many political and constitutional cases which highlighted the struggle for independence, I had a rare opportunity to follow at close range the dramatic events of those days. When at last the British Government decided to grant independence to Sierra Leone and a Constitutional All Party Independence Conference was convened at Lancaster House in London, I was one of the three who represented the People's National Party at that Conference. The other two, Albert Margai and Siaka Stevens, have since attained supreme power as Prime Ministers of Sierra Leone, the latter succeeding the former after an intervening period of military rule.

As head of Sierra Leone's Permanent Mission at the United Nations from the achievement of independence in September 1961 to October 1963 and again from May 1964 to January 1967, I was in continuous contact with my country's debut into international affairs. From October 1963 to January 1967 I was also Ambassador to the United States. When in 1967 I returned home to become Chief Justice I had a unique opportunity to observe at very close range the events that directly led to the breakdown of the democratic process and constitutional government in Sierra Leone.

These experiences, I hope, have given me a certain qualification to comment on and perhaps interpret the story of Sierra Leone's first experiment with democracy after its colonial era.

## NOTES

1. Quoted in Roy Lewis, *Sierra Leone* (London, H.M. Stationery Office, 1954), p. 2.
2. The other two countries are Ghana and Nigeria.

# Sierra Leone

# CHAPTER 1

# Early Constitutional and Political Development, 1787-1951

Modern organized government in Sierra Leone may be said to have come into existence in 1787 with the settlement of hundreds of freed and destitute slaves in the peninsula area.[1] This peninsula area however, was only a small part of what is now Sierra Leone, the rest of the territory as will be explained later, was acquired over a century afterwards in 1896 when the British proclaimed a Protectorate in the much larger adjoining land. Even though this early attempt at modern government was rather timid, limited, and essentially communal, it was meant to meet the exigencies of the peculiar situation.

It is interesting to note that from the start, Granville Sharp, the British philanthropist whose exertions had made the experiment possible, intended the settlers to enjoy self-government. In Sierra Leone, Sharp "looked to provide a country and a constitution." [2] He advised the settlers to govern themselves on the basis of "a constitution, bound by a social contract, rooted in history, in the institutions of the Anglo-Saxon monarchy, and of Israel under the judges. Its bond was the old English system of Frankpledge. Every ten householders would form a tithing, every ten tithings a hundred collectively responsible for preserving order and keeping watch against outside enemies, each householder with a voice in a Common Council." [3]

Though these early settlers had sworn allegiance to the King of England before leaving England for Sierra Leone, when once the settlement was established, they became free settlers in the land which Sharp loved to call the "Province of Freedom." [4]

On their arrival in Sierra Leone in 1787, the settlers put into effect their plans for self-government by electing governing officials including a Chief in Command or Governor.[5] Soon afterwards land was purchased for the settlement and an organized community was constituted whose members hoped to rule themselves without reference to higher authority. But this first period of self-government and virtual independence was not destined to last, for in 1790 the indigenous Temne tribe burnt the first settlement.

The indefatigable Granville Sharp however, did not despair. He solicited in England for additional funds to restore the settlement. This time, he found it necessary to supplement his original philanthropic arguments with economic ones. Later, when some hundred promoters successfully petitioned the British parliament for the incorporation of a company, greater emphasis was put on commercial than on philanthropic intentions.[6]

This was a period in European imperialism when European powers particularly the British, felt they had a right to acquire and extend their suzerainty over remote territories all over the world. And so the Sierra Leone Company was incorporated in London in 1791 with authority "to hold from the Crown, the land originally granted, and any other land they might acquire on the peninsula." [7] This act vested management in thirteen directors, elected annually by the shareholders. It also conferred on the Company powers to make laws until the settlers were capable of making their own.

The incorporation of the Sierra Leone Company in 1791 brought to an end the self-government of the new Province of Freedom. Active control of the settlers passed on to absentee directors who gave instructions from London to their representative in Sierra Leone, the Governor. The Sierra Leone Company had to wait, however, until 1800 before receiving the charter by which the territory was formally constituted a colony with the Company's directors exercising the same kind of control exercised by the Secretary of State in British colonies.

Under the Charter of 1800, there were a governor and councillors appointed by the Company in London. They sat in Freetown as judges, with a jury system, in the trial of criminal cases. Freetown itself became a municipal corporation with a mayor and alderman who sat as judges, with juries, to try civil cases. These officials were not elected, but were appointed by the Governor and council.[8]

It was a period in the constitutional story of Sierra Leone

marked by frustrations and disappointments—not only on the part of the philanthropists and promoters who had sponsored the settlement, but also on the part of the settlers themselves. The shareholders of the Sierra Leone Company had hoped at least for what they considered fair, if not necessarily quick, returns on their investments in the colony. The colony yielded hardly anything measurable in financial terms to compensate them for their efforts and investments. The settlers steadfastly refused even to pay rent for the land allotted them. They had arrived in Sierra Leone with the highest hopes for freedom and a determination not to tolerate any situation remotely reminiscent of the slavery and oppression they had left behind. They did not scruple to oppose the Company's rule whenever they believed their dignity and freedom threatened. This opposition was taken to the point of open rebellion in 1800 when their leaders sought to supplement the authority of the Company by their own published Code of Laws.[9] The basic position of the settlers at this time was that they owned the land, that only their own elected representatives had the right to make laws, and that all foreigners should pay taxes to them.[10] Even though the Company was able to use superior military force to enforce its authority, the fundamental approach of the settlers never really changed.

The Sierra Leone Company, however, was soon quite happy to transfer its responsibilities for the colony to the British Crown. In 1808 the constitutional status of Sierra Leone changed from a colony of an incorporated company to that of crown colony. Through this transfer the administrative authority of the directors passed to the British Secretary of State.[11]

The 1808 change did not at first make much difference in the life of the settlers. They were spared military rule, and most of the constitutional provisions enjoyed under the Company's charter, including jury trial, were preserved under the new status. During this period, the executive powers of the governor were very great. In those days of sailing ships it took at least a month for dispatches to reach him from London. He was therefore in almost complete control and left free to conduct his own policies.

In 1821, an act was passed in the British Parliament which abolished the African Company for the Gold Coast Forts (the company that had supervised up to that time all British Government interests in that part of West Africa) and transferred to the British

Crown its dependencies. By this act all the dependencies as well as all other British possessions in West Africa between 20° north and 20° south latitude, became dependencies of Sierra Leone. This area included the territories of the Gold Coast (now Ghana), Sierra Leone, and the Gambia. A new constitution was drawn up in 1821 which increased the Governor's Council from three to nine members. This number included two stationed in the Gold Coast. Under the new constitutional provisions, the Freetown Court of Recorder was given jurisdiction on cases from all the dependencies, with two members of Council sitting with the Chief Justice as Assistant Judges. The mayor and aldermen lost their former judicial powers. Important features of this 1821 constitution were the right of veto in Council and the rank of Chancellor given to the Governor, which empowered him to hear chancery cases.[12]

In 1827, the united government of the Gold Coast, Sierra Leone, and the Gambia was disjoined. This brought to an end the executive, although not the legislative, authority of the governor and council in Sierra Leone over the Gold Coast and the Gambia.[13]

The 1821 constitution had remained essentially unamended. Even though Sierra Leoneans were taxed, they had no representation whatever in the government. The only method then available to them for expressing their views was through petitions, and these they increasingly used.

In 1863, following a petition in 1853,[14] a new constitution was introduced. Though the petition for direct elections was rejected, the new constitution could be said to mark an improvement for Sierra Leone. For the first time an African, John Ezzidio, was nominated to be a member of the Legislative Council, with a clear mandate to be the spokesman for the interests of merchants who were predominantly Creole.[15] This development could hardly be regarded as the beginning of true representative government in Sierra Leone since the British Government insisted that Ezzidio was not a delegate but a nominee of the merchants, removable at the Queen's pleasure and not at the pleasure of the merchants.

The 1863 constitution provided for an Executive Council comprising the Governor, the Chief Justice, the Queen's Advocate, the Colonial Secretary, and the officer commanding the troops. It also provided for a Legislative Council consisting of all the members of the Executive Council with additional unofficial members appointed by the Governor and confirmed by the Secretary of State.[16] The additional unofficial members included one African to represent the mercantile community. The new constitution, however, was essentially a device for the more efficient government of an expanding colony, rather than a concession to the principle of representation.

In 1866 a new constitutional amendment was adopted unifying the West African Settlement of Sierra Leone, the Gambia, the Gold Coast, and Nigeria with Freetown as headquarters.[17] This step was taken in the hope that administration would thereby become easier and cheaper. Within ten years, however, the new arrangements were found to be inefficient and generally unsatisfactory and accordingly were abandoned in 1874.[18] The Gambia continued to be administered jointly with Sierra Leone, as the West African Settlements, from Freetown. In 1889 the two countries were finally disjoined and Sierra Leone was ruled separately, and was still governed by the 1863 constitution, which gave Creoles only token representation. When the constitution was first implemented, only one Creole, John Ezzidio, had been appointed. Later, in 1869, appointment of another Creole, William Grant, increased the nominated representation to two. Even this token representation was limited in 1895 to a five-year term. It was deprived of much meaning in 1896 on the appointment of an Attorney General.[19] From then on, debates in the Legislative Council became merely formal adoptions of decisions already reached in the Executive Council after deliberations in that chamber and introduced into the Legislative Council by the Attorney General. This led to the stifling by the official members of debates that they resented as personal criticisms.

In 1896, the British Government established a protectorate over extensive land adjoining the colony. The Foreign Jurisdiction Act of 1890, which consolidated a series of earlier acts, had authorized the British Crown to exercise "any jurisdiction claimed in a foreign country as if by right of cession or conquest." Following the promulgation of this act, the British Government acquired jurisdiction in what they then described as "foreign countries adjoining the Colony." [20] Thus the British proclaimed the Sierra Leone Protectorate in 1896 without much prior consultation with the people of the area even though they declared at the time that it was "best for the interests of the people." [21]

When the coastal Temne tribe ceded a strip of land to the British in 1787, they never could have guessed that this simple act would lead a century later to the loss of their entire land to the alien British. In fact, it is highly doubtful whether the illiterate and inexperienced Temnes knew what they were selling or what the real nature was of the transaction they had been party to. The boundaries of Sierra Leone were settled with neither the knowledge nor the consent of the people whose land was involved. Rather, these boundaries were settled on the south by the then weak and inexperienced Liberian Government and the much stronger and demanding British [22] and on the north and the northeast by the British and the French who were at that time establishing their territorial claims over neighboring Guinea.[23]

The proclamation of a protectorate by the British Government over the hinterland of Sierra Leone was the culminating act in a policy of ruthless expansionism which they had embarked upon ever since the area of the colony was declared a Crown Colony in 1808. This policy which was one of intimidation as well as one of expansion at first developed slowly. But by 1876 it had gained momentum. Punitive expeditions into the hinterland to overawe any recalcitrant chief became quite common. Military interventions in intertribal warfare were events of frequent occurrence.[24] The Colony governors now and again undertook through the use of force to install nominees of their choice as chiefs of neighboring tribes after they had deposed legitimate rulers of the people. Both the Creoles of the Colony and the Europeans who had settled in the Colony persisted in extending their trade and influence throughout the hinterland. The British had gradually extended their territorial acquisition in Sierra Leone through treaties, cession, and compulsory annexation. This extension of British influence soon rendered unimportant the frontier between the Colony and the hinterland. Inevitably, clashes occurred and quite often the British were routed by the indigenous tribes. By and large, however, they continued their relentless advance toward the complete subjugation of the whole area.

To complicate the situation further, the French had embarked on a trade and territorial expansionist policy which threatened to interfere with the Colony's markets in the hinterland of Sierra Leone. The British therefore believed it vital to their interests to bring the whole hinterland under British protection and influence as soon as possible.[25]

The term "protectorate," [26] which was first used in the Berlin Conference of 1885, had not even been defined at the time of the annexation in 1896.[27] It was left to the British to arbitrarily determine its scope. So when it became apparent to them that to ensure more efficient exploitation of the economic, agricultural, material, and human resources of the hinterland, this area should be annexed, they proceeded to do just that.

Although an Order in Council passed in 1895 authorized the Sierra Leone Legislative Council to legislate for the Protectorate in the same way as for the Colony,[28] the British administrators, from the inception of the Protectorate, displayed an awareness of the authority of chieftancy and other indigenous institutions in tribal life. Accordingly, they introduced a system of government and administration that was calculated to preserve tribal institutions within a larger framework rather than to be in conflict with them.

For purposes of administration, the Protectorate was divided into five districts, each under the jurisdiction of a District Commissioner. The District Commissioner shared power in his district with the Paramount Chief, the term used to describe a principal chief with chiefs and subchiefs in his chiefdom. While the Paramount Chiefs continued to preside over minor cases in which citizens of the Protectorate were involved, matters relating to serious crimes came before the District Commissioner. It was the District Commissioner who had jurisdiction in the Protectorate over persons who were not indigenous citizens of that area, and over cases of "native slave dealing, witchcraft, land cases between Paramount Chiefs, and cases arising from tribal fights." [29]

Whereas in the Colony the English common law and legal procedures were in full use, in the Protectorate the District Commissioner was guided by English legal procedures but not bound by them. The District Commissioner had powers to administer summary justice in the Protectorate based on "common sense rather than legal precedents" (see note 27).

The development of society and the expansion of the economy in the Protectorate soon made it necessary for the British to introduce modifications to the Protectorate Ordinance of 1896. For example, before long it became clear that the traditional authority of chiefs within the framework of British Protectorate administration should be strengthened to enable them to perform a wider set of functions in keeping with the changes that annexation had brought. To put muscle into the administration by traditional authorities, the British

Government gradually introduced isolated measures in the fields of finance, sanitation, medical services, road building, agriculture, and education.

Unlike the Colony, the Protectorate was not subject to frequent statutory constitutional changes after its establishment. However, further rethinking of policy for the Protectorate led the British to overhaul the basis of Protectorate administration. Much later, in 1937, following the model known as "Native Administration," a system of indirect rule which Lord Lugard had made famous in Nigeria,[30] the British formally introduced a new system at which time eighteen separate administrations were instituted.

Under Native Administration, sweeping innovations were introduced into Protectorate administration which no doubt advanced the modernization process of this part of the country. The new measures strengthened the traditional sources of authority and the power of the chiefs. However, in spite of the advantages of this system of indirect rule, it was essentially a network of administration primarily suitable for the control of indigenous and tribal populations in a colonial context.

After the establishment of the Protectorate in 1896, Sierra Leone comprised for all administrative purposes both the Colony and the Protectorate. The Governor in Freetown presided over both areas with near-dictatorial powers exercised through the Executive Council and the Legislative Council as provided for under the 1863 Constitution. However, although control of the Protectorate was exercised from the Colony from the time of annexation in 1896, it was not until 1913 that the Legislative Council in Freetown actually legislated for both the Colony and the Protectorate.

In 1924 a new constitution was introduced. This constitution also provided for a Governor, a Legislative Council, and an Executive Council, but with the councils differently constituted.[31] The constitutional situation these new provisions were to replace was a Legislative Council with six official members including the Governor and four nominated unofficial members—three Africans and one European. It is important to note that "official" members were civil servants holding important offices as heads of departments who were ex-officio members of the Council. "Nominated" members were persons appointed by the Governor.

The 1924 Constitution provided for a Legislative Council with twelve official members and ten unofficial members. The twelve official members all sat on the government benches and took their seats "ex-officio." [32] Even at this stage of the country's development very little homage was paid to democratic principles by the British. Only three of the ten unofficial members were elected, and these were from the Colony. Two other colonial representatives sat on the Council through direct nomination by the Governor. The Protectorate was represented by three Paramount Chiefs nominated by the Governor— two from the Mendes and one from the Temnes. Two nominated Europeans representing commercial and general European interests completed the number of unofficial membership of the new Legislative Council.[33] In a council of twenty-two members, only eight were Africans, and only three of these were elected.

The new Constitution also provided for an Executive Council similar in scope and complexion to the then-existing Executive Council. It continued to be presided over by the Governor and had an exclusively colonial membership without any African representation. From the point of view of the development of unitary government in Sierra Leone, the 1924 constitution was a landmark in the country's constitutional history. By its provision for the representation of the Protectorate through nominated chiefs in the same legislature with Colony representatives, the constitution sought to vest statutory authority in the joint administration of the Colony and the Protectorate.[34]

It is significant that the Creoles in the Colony stoutly resisted the introduction of the 1924 constitution. They used all kinds of arguments, including legal ones, to support their opposition. Their behavior seemed motivated by several considerations. First, they argued that the chiefs were too susceptible to the influences of the local colonial administration to make them much more than willing puppets of the colonial officials. In support of this contention, they cited the provision enabling Provincial Commissioners (who had overlord authority over all District Commissioners in their Province) or District Commissioners to sit in the Legislative Council concurrently with chiefs, not only to advise them but also to speak on their behalf. The Creoles' main point was that since in the Protectorate the District Commissioners exercised undue influence over the chiefs, the presence of the chiefs in the Council in such circumstances would have the effect only of enlarging the official colonial representation.[35]

Second, the Colony Creoles argued, the method of nominating chiefs did not guarantee that they truly represented either their own people or their brother chiefs. As a matter of fact, at the time this particular constitutional debate was being conducted, relations between chiefs and people were greatly strained because of alleged misuse of chiefly powers. For their third argument against the nomination of chiefs to the Legislative Council, the Colony Creoles relied on a legalistic nicety. They claimed that since the Legislative Council was instituted originally as the legislature of the Colony of Sierra Leone, whose citizens were British subjects, it was illegal to appoint any African from the Protectorate to sit in such a legislature. They referred to the Foreign Jurisdiction Act of 1890 which established that British-protected persons were aliens; being aliens, the argument ran, such British-protected persons could not legislate for British subjects.[36]

The 1924 constitution was implemented in spite of the vigorous opposition of the Colony Creoles. However, the Colony representatives in the new Legislative Council used the greater strength provided them under the new constitution to criticize government policies and persistently demand a stronger voice in the affairs of government.

In due course, the Colonial Government yielded two important concessions. In November 1938, it established a Standing Finance Committee of the Legislature consisting of two official members (the Colonial Secretary and the Colonial Treasurer) and all the unofficial members (seven Africans and three Europeans).[37] The establishment of this Finance Committee of the Legislative Council marked a distinct advance in constitutional government in Sierra Leone, as it enabled Africans for the first time, to keep a stricter check on supplementary expenditure after the passing of the budget and to experience the satisfaction of actually controlling a majority in an important government committee.

The second concession, and by far the more important, was the appointment in 1943 of two Africans to the Executive Council, one from the Colony and the other from the Protectorate. Since the Executive Council was the supreme policy-making organ of government, this development was of historic significance as it gave Africans for the first time the opportunity not only of influencing policy, but of getting a close-up view of the processes at work in the formulation of policy.

The real decolonization process in Sierra Leone started in 1947 when the British authorities submitted new constitutional proposals. Immediately prior to the presentation of these proposals, the British authorities established the Protectorate Assembly in 1945–46.[38] It was their expressed view that before granting Africans more control of the affairs of government, the Protectorate section of the country should be helped and encouraged to rectify the imbalance of progress between the Colony and the Protectorate. The establishment of the Protectorate Assembly in 1945–46 was apparently intended to provide a framework for surmounting the political and social backwardness existing in the Protectorate.

The Protectorate (Amendment) Ordinance which gave birth to the Protectorate Assembly provided for a membership of forty-two. Twenty-six of these seats were reserved for Paramount Chiefs indirectly elected to the Assembly by native administrations and district councils. Eleven of the seats were reserved for government department officials. Of the remaining members, one was to represent European business interests, one Creole business interests, and one missionary interests. Two seats were reserved for educated Protectorate Africans selected by Native Administrations.

It should be noted that in giving democratic opportunities to the Protectorate the British authorities acted as though they believed that the chiefs were the only relevant representatives of the people. This conclusion becomes inevitable when one considers the exclusive nomination of chiefs as representatives of the Protectorate in the Legislative Council and the preponderance of chiefs in the new Protectorate Assembly, quite apart from their overwhelming role in the administration through the district-council and native-administration systems. This preference for chiefs as representatives of the people was later bound to lead to conflicts between the chiefs and the educated elements in the Protectorate. In 1950, largely because of pressures from the latter group, the number of seats reserved for representatives who were neither chiefs nor officials was raised from two to six.

The new constitutional proposals that the British Government presented in 1947 marked great progress in the constitutional development of Sierra Leone as for the first time they would lead to an unofficial and African majority in the legislature.[39]

First, the membership of the legislature was enlarged to twenty-four—sixteen to be unofficial members and eight official. The Governor, as one of the official members, was to continue as President of the Council. Perhaps by far the most significant development was that provision was made for an African majority as fourteen of the sixteen unofficial members were to be Africans and the other two Europeans. Under the conditions then existing in the civil service, it was the natural assumption that the eight official members would be Europeans.

The 1947 proposals fell far short of a full application of democratic principles. For example, only four of the fourteen unofficial African members of the Legislative Council were to be elected by direct franchise and these were to represent only Colony constituencies. The other ten unofficial members were to represent Protectorate interests. Of these members, nine were to be elected by the Protectorate Assembly dominated by the chiefs and one nominated by the Governor from among the members of the same Protectorate Assembly. In this difference in the types of franchise exercisable in the two areas, one finds another instance of the application of two separate systems in the territory.

Not surprisingly, the Colony leaders strongly opposed the 1947 constitutional proposals. They saw in them a blatant attempt on the part of the British authorities to impose Protectorate leadership, since the new constitution gave so many more seats to the Protectorate and ensured for it a built-in majority.

It seemed that the British expected a discussion to develop between leaders of both sections of the country in the hope that differences would be resolved and compromises reached. Unfortunately, the mood of both sides was not such as to produce any worthwhile consensus. What developed instead was a bitter and acrimonious debate between them, a debate in which surfaced the worst aspects of the tribal animosities which are always latent in Sierra Leone politics.

The Creoles of the Colony vehemently argued that "illiterates" should not be allowed to be members of the same legislature as Colony members and use the majority thus acquired to legislate for them. In a spirited dispatch to the Secretary of State for the Colonies, following a public meeting in Freetown in 1948, the Creoles disparaged the people of the Protectorate as "foreigners" and stated gingerly that ". . . a legislative Council in the Colony with a majority of foreigners, as British protected persons are in the Commonwealth, is contrary to the whole conception of British citizens. British citizens have the right that they shall be governed only by such persons as are of the same status as themselves. . . . By the suggested set-up of Protectorate majority, persons who are not British subjects would be empowered to make legislation that may seriously affect the rights of British subjects. . . ." [40]

The Creoles relentlessly kept up the pressures against the new proposals through the press, political activities, delegations to London, and lawsuits challenging their constitutionality. The Protectorate leaders, on the other hand, welcomed them. At first the newly emerging educated elements in the Protectorate were inclined to resent the power the chiefs were to enjoy under the new proposals; eventually, all Protectorate groups rallied and gave their undivided support, largely due, no doubt, to the vehemence and the tribal overtones of the attacks from the Colony.

In response to the demands of the Colony leaders, the Protectorate leaders agreed that the Colony representation in the new Legislative Council be increased from four to seven by the addition of three seats, with the understanding that the Protectorate representation should also be increased by three seats, bringing their membership to thirteen. However, on the second demand of the Colony leaders that all members of the new legislature should be literate, the Protectorate leaders refused to yield ground. They stubbornly rejected the Colony case and adhered to their position that literacy as such should not be considered a *sine qua non* for parliamentary representation.

After an inconclusive public debate, with neither side yielding any significant ground, the British colonial Government announced its intention of implementing the 1947 proposals.[41] Unfortunately, the three years of acrimonious debate over the constitutional proposals left their mark on relations between the Colony and the Protectorate. Not only had the Colony leaders attacked the Protectorate peoples as foreigners, but the Protectorate leaders had also scathingly described the Colony Creoles as ". . . a handful of foreigners . . . that our forefathers had given shelter . . . who have no will to cooperate with us and imagine themselves to be our superiors because they are aping the Western mode of living, and have never breathed the true spirit of independence. . . ." [42]

This development was particularly unfortunate as it poisoned the relationship between the two major groups in the country and deprived Sierra Leone of a valuable public discussion of fundamental questions, including the protection of minority interests, at a time when the course of the nation was being irrevocably set toward independence. The Protectorate leaders, fully aware of their strength in numbers and stung by the vehemence and virulence of the Colony attacks, were in no mood for compromises. The position was clearly expressed in a speech by Dr. Milton Margai, the leader of the Protectorate group, before the Protectorate Assembly in 1950 when he said, "Feelings have run so high on both sides that no useful purpose will be served by sitting with them in a committee just now. . . . If the 30,000 non-natives in the Colony should attempt a boycott, I make no hesitation to assure the Government that all of the seats on the Colony side would be occupied by our countrymen. We mean to push ahead and we are in no way prepared to allow a handful of foreigners to impede our progress." [43]

In 1951, the 1947 proposals—with minor modifications by the Governor's Order in Council—became law and the 1924 constitution was revoked. Thus Sierra Leone had a new constitution with a framework of representative government. The scene was now set, with an African unofficial majority at last, for Sierra Leone to embark on the road to political independence.

## NOTES

1. Landing made on May 10, 1787; treaty concluded by King Tom and Subchiefs Pa Bongee and Queen Yamacouba on June 11, 1787 (Admiralty-Captain Lon, 627, p. 25, May 6, 1787; and Treasury Board Papers, 645, 968.).

2. Christopher Fyfe, *A History of Sierra Leone,* Oxford Univ. Press (1962), p. 16.

3. *Ibid.*

4. On their request, parchments signed by the Clerk of the Acts of the Navy were given to the settlers, granting them the status of free settlers in the Province of Freedom. See Admiralty–Navy Board in letter 2347, December 4, 1886. See also Treasury Board Papers, 636, 2430.

5. Richard Weaver was chosen as the governor. Treasury Board Papers, 487, 643.

6. For debate on the bill to incorporate a company, see Commons Journal, Vol. XI, pp. 405, 414, 442, 454 ff.

7. Act. 31, Geo. III, Cap. 55.

8. Minutes of Governor's Council, Nov. 8, 1800.

9. Colonial Office Minutes of Councils. Vol. V, pp. 98–110.

10. Minutes of Governor's Council, Sept. 10, 1799 and Dec. 16–20, 1799.

11. 47 Geo. III sess. 11, Cap. 44 (1808).

12. Montague, *The Ordinances of Sierra Leone,* Vol. III, pp. 153–56.

13. Dispatch to and from Secretary of State, Ricketts Lieutenant Governor, June 25, 1828; Huskisson Secretary of State, Dec. 8, 1827; and Jeremie Governor, 1841, 8 Min.

14. Petition from Mercantile Association to Secretary of State. Governor's dispatch to Secretary of State, Hill, 1858, No. 29; Hill, 1858, No. 50 enc.

15. Governor's dispatch to Secretary of State Rogers, Blackhall 1863, 152, and Blackhall July 21, 1863.

16. Montague, *Ordinances of Sierra Leone,* Vol. III, pp. 193–96.

17. Montague, *Ordinances of Sierra Leone,* Vol. III, p. 197.

18. Parliamentary Debates (iii), Vol. CCXIX, pp. 159–60.

19. Executive Council Debate for May 1896.

20. For Foreign Jurisdiction Act of 1890, see (a) 53 and 54 Vic. Cap. 37, Order-in-Council of August 28, 1895; (b) *Government Gazette* for August 31, 1896.

21. See note 20 (b).

22. Christopher Fyfe, *History of Sierra Leone,* p. 540.

23. Parliamentary Papers 1899, Vol. IX. See the Chalmers Report, Vol. I, pp. 11, 15.

24. Little, *Mende of Sierra Leone,* p. 43.

25. The British and French Governments signed an agreement on January 21, 1895 at Paris, fixing the lines along which the boundaries were to be demarcated.

26. At the trial of James Raid in London, the Lord Chief Justice stated that "Protectorates vary infinitely." *Times* (London), July 29, 1896.

27. Christopher Fyfe, *History of Sierra Leone,* p. 542.

28. See note 20 (b).

29. Parliamentary Papers 1899, Vol. IX, the Chalmers Report, Vol. II, pp. 543, 544; and Protectorate Ordinances 20 of 1896; 11 of 1897 and 15 of 1897.

30. Margery Perham, *Native Administration in Nigeria.*

31. Legislative Council Debates, Dec. 1922.

32. Sierra Leone (Legislative Council) Order in Council, January 1924.

33. *Ibid.*

34. *Ibid.*

35. Legislative Council Debates No. II, 1923–1924.

36. See note 20 (a).

37. Legislative Council Debates No. I, 1939–1940.

38. Legislative Council Debates, 1944–1945.

39. "Proposals for the Reconstitution of the Legislative Council of Sierra Leone," No. II of 1948.

40. Memorandum presented to the Secretary of State for the Colonies by Political Organizations of the Colony (1948).

41. Sierra Leone Legislative Council Debates: 1949–50.

42. Speech of Dr. Milton Margai, first Prime Minister of independent Sierra Leone, before the Seventh Protectorate Assembly.

43. *Ibid.*

# CHAPTER 2

# Decade Before Independence— Constitution and Politics, 1951-1961

When once the 1951 Constitution had been implemented, the British Government made it abundantly clear that it had every intention of honoring its commitment to grant political independence to the country as soon as possible. This willingness after 1951 on the part of the British to facilitate progress toward independence in Sierra Leone constituted a most remarkable feature in the Anglo-Sierra Leonean relationship. The entire record of the struggle for independence in Sierra Leone since the nineteen-forties glows with evidence of this friendly cooperation between the government and the governed. Sierra Leone's march toward independence was singularly free from the bitterness and conflict which highlighted relationships in many other African territories. Whether this aspect of the constitutional story of Sierra Leone was a blessing or not, it certainly set the tone for the nonmilitant, acquiescent, and almost apologetic nationalism that characterized Sierra Leone's early years of independence.

During the first year of the implementation of the 1951 Constitution, the Governor granted African members of the Executive Council ministerial portfolios. At this stage, the offer was little more than a political gesture confining responsibilities purely to the sphere of administration. Real policy making was still left in the hands of the British Government. However, it definitely marked a decisive forward step in the political development of the country. For the first time, Africans were able to enjoy a superior status over European expatriate officials in the administration and government. The fact and reality of political power was brought home very forcibly to the people by an African majority not only in the Legislative Council but also in the Executive Council.

The transfer of power from the British Colonial authorities to Sierra Leoneans continued with unimpeded momentum after 1951. The nominal grant in 1951 of portfolios to African members of the Executive Council was quickly followed in 1953 by the grant of real authority for policy making. On this date, the leader of the Africans in the Executive Council, Dr. Milton Margai,[1] was appointed Chief Minister.

With the appointment of a Sierra Leonean as Chief Minister and the designation of other Sierra Leoneans in the Executive Council as Ministers, Sierra Leone entered a new political era. Leading Sierra Leonean politicians of the majority party abandoned the nationalist politicians' classical role of would-be revolutionaries, ever watchful and critical of government policy and seemingly anxious to change the order of things. Such posture, which had much to recommend it during the days when sole responsibility for government policy resided with the British authorities, immediately lost its validity now that the British were sharing the policy-making role with Sierra Leonean leaders. In fact, the participation of Sierra Leonean politicians in the sphere of policy making became overly obvious and exaggerated by the designation of these leaders as Ministers and by their actual holding of portfolios in their new authoritative positions.

The political leaders in command of the majority party [2] now embarked on an active policy of cooperation with the British colonial authorities and gradually assumed the role of apologists if not outright defenders of British colonial policy from 1953 until independence in 1961. The tasks of opposition, including criticism of British colonial policy, became then the prerogative of the other parties and groups in and out of the legislature. In the Legislative Council, opposition was led by the experienced and redoubtable Dr. H. C. Bankole-Bright, a Creole politician of great durability and resourcefulness who waged a fierce and unsuccessful struggle to resist the advance of popular democracy in Sierra Leone.[3] This was the period that saw the desperate gasping efforts of the Colony Creoles to preserve a special and separate political identity outside a body politic which included the Protectorate.

In spite of the new role of power and authority conferred on Sierra Leonean ministers as members of the Cabinet holding portfolios, the real strings of power were still left largely in the hands of expatriate department heads who were later to be designated as Permanent Secretaries. As the new arrangements did not provide for an African minister to be in charge of every department of government, there were some departments that continued with expatriates in full control without any African ministerial supervision. Even in the case of those departments that had African ministers supervising policy, there were expatriate department heads who wielded great influence in policy formation and had complete control of the administrative machinery. As a matter of fact, the more important and sensitive areas of government in Sierra Leone remained under the effective authority and control of expatriate British officials, not only for administrative purposes but also for policy making.[4] More significant was the fact that certain department heads in important departments continued membership in the Legislative Council and shared there the responsibility with African ministers for the defense of government policy.[5] The Governor kept the responsibility for the Public Service in his own hands even though at that time (1953) the British had accepted a policy of rapid Africanization to ensure an indigenous civil service after independence.

During this transition period, the British Government sought to justify its policy of keeping expatriate British control of so many important areas of government by pointing out that Sierra Leoneans were not sufficiently trained in technical and administrative skills to ensure efficient government otherwise. The British also advanced the further argument that African ministers needed time to prepare themselves for the exercise of ministerial responsibility.

In pursuit of the policy that Africans had to be prepared and trained, certain areas of government responsibility including the Public Service, the Judiciary, Finance, Foreign Affairs, and Defense at this stage were left under the direct control of the Colonial Governor. He continued after 1953—until 1960, a year before independence—to discharge these responsibilities. In the case of the Public Service, he delegated his authority to the chairman of the new Public Service Commission, an expatriate. In the areas of finance and foreign policy, the Governor kept ultimate responsibility and continued to delegate some of the responsibilities for finance to a Financial Secretary, also an expatriate British official.[6]

During this period, it became the British official policy to accelerate the training of Sierra Leoneans to assume responsibilities of government in technical and administrative fields. On the higher levels this aim was accomplished mainly through training in the United Kingdom. About this period also, countries friendly to Britain—such as the United States, France, Canada, Australia, and other Commonwealth countries—offered a limited number of overseas scholarships in this effort to prepare Sierra Leoneans to assume the responsibilities of independence.

Internally, much was being done within the limits of the country's resources to prepare for independence. In the field of education the Government now embarked on a vigorous program of school building. Scholarship awards for secondary education were multiplied several times from the numbers awarded in colonial days. The Government displayed a growing awareness and concern for Africanizing the public services. The government information agencies as represented by the Department of Information and the Sierra Leone Broadcasting Service were refurbished. Fourah Bay College, a university college with more than a century's relationship with Durham University in England and renowned for its distinguished services to education throughout West Africa, at last came into its own and enjoyed complete government sponsorship and support.

Thus, the development of Sierra Leone had arrived at a stage in the nineteen-fifties when African leaders had begun to exercise a decisive influence in the formulation and implementation of government policy. Africans at last had come within striking range of controlling the destiny of Sierra Leone. This was the period of internal self-government when most areas of internal policy were controlled from Freetown and not from Whitehall in London. But what was without doubt of greatest significance at this time was the fact that this African participation in government was conducted from a unicameral legislature where Protectorate and Colony leaders were speaking in the name of a united Sierra Leone including both the Colony and the Protectorate. Even though the voices of separatist Colony opposition had not been completely silenced, they had been effectively muted. The peoples of Sierra Leone at this time were ready for independence.

By the end of 1959, it was well known in political circles in Sierra Leone that independence was imminent. The British Government made it quite clear that it was ready to cooperate with Sierra Leoneans for the achievement of independence.

The scene was finally set for the Independence All Party Constitutional talks in London in 1960 and the feverish political atmosphere which prevailed in Sierra Leone during the period immediately preceding independence and at the advent of independence.

## NOTES

1. Later Sir Milton Margai.
2. S.L.P.P. (Sierra Leone People's Party).
3. Dr. Bankole-Bright was the leader of the N.C.C.S.L. (National Council for the Colony of Sierra Leone) formed August 1950 with almost exclusively Creole colony membership.
4. The Public Service, Judiciary, and Departments of Finance, Defense, and External Affairs.
5. Such department heads were the Director of Medical Services, the Director of Education, and the Director of Agriculture.
6. The Sierra Leone Government continued for several years after independence to use an expatriate British official as Head of the Finance Department.

# CHAPTER 3

# The Politics of Independence, 1961

After the 1951 Constitution had been in operation for nearly ten years, it was quite clear to all that complete constitutional independence for Sierra Leone could not be much further delayed. With the prevailing political mood in British West Africa, Sierra Leone, for all her proud reputation of loyalty to the British throne, could not remain unaffected by the winds of political change that were sweeping through the continent.

In 1959 and 1960, in the atmosphere of independence prevalent among British colonial territories in West Africa, it seemed at last that Sierra Leone's time had come. Ghana, the former colonial territory of the Gold Coast, had blazed the trail of independence in sub-Sahara Africa. After an energetic and dramatic confrontation with the British, Kwame Nkrumah, by the achievement of independence for Ghana in 1957, had clearly demonstrated that independence for African countries was no longer a myth but an exciting reality. Nigeria, a country with which Sierra Leone had always enjoyed the most friendly relations and generous mutual admiration, had followed Ghana into independence in 1960 under less dramatic circumstances. Only the Gambia and Sierra Leone continued as British colonies in West Africa after 1960.

Quite apart from the well-publicized events from sister British colonies, there were the equally loud noises from neighboring countries already independent—Liberia and Guinea. Liberia, a republic which had achieved independence more than a century earlier (1847), was calmly and placidly pursuing her well-established political freedom. Guinea, on the other hand, led by the dynamic and fire-eating Sekou Toure, excited the envy and admiration of many in Sierra Leone. The sheer defiance, originality, courage, and nationalist bravado of the man had made a great impression on Sierra Leoneans. All had applauded his 1958 defiance of de Gaulle and the French when he led his people to vote "No" in the French Constitutional Referendum and thereby chose immediate independence. As a matter of fact, after the independence of Ghana in 1957 and of Nigeria in 1960, the British seemed to have reconciled themselves to the fact that their remaining colonies in West Africa could no longer be frustrated in their quest for independence.

Immediately prior to independence, there was a great outburst of political party activities in Sierra Leone which assuredly was not unrelated to the certainty of impending independence. Politicians considered it to be of the most crucial importance that their respective groups should enjoy the distinction of leading the country into independence. They were also fully aware of the strategic advantages derivable from wresting control of the levers of power at this particular juncture and the possibility of using these levers for the preservation of a particular group in power after independence.

The majority party in the legislature and also in the country at large was the Sierra Leone People's Party (S.L.P.P.). The S.L.P.P. had been formed in April 1951 in the immediate aftermath of the constitutional proposals of 1947 and the great national debate that followed the publication of these proposals. Its establishment came in direct response to the activities of the National Council for the Colony of Sierra Leone, a predominantly Creole-oriented group dedicated to the expression and preservation of exclusively Creole interests. As a counterforce, the S.L.P.P. was intended to be the party to represent, defend, and advance Protectorate interests. True, the party had as its motto "One People, One Country," yet it was quite clear that in the context of the Sierra Leone of the times the achievement of the aims in the party's motto could only be ensured through rectifying the imbalance in development between the Colony and the Protectorate.

The leadership of the S.L.P.P. was in the hands of two brothers, Milton and Albert Margai. Dr. Milton Margai,[1] the chairman and parliamentary leader, was closely associated with the chiefs and the tribal ruling elite of the Protectorate. Albert Margai,[2] the younger brother, was the darling of the young educated elements in the Protectorate now staking their claims for a share in the conduct of national affairs.

The main opposition party in the Legislative Council had been the United Progressive People's Party (U.P.P.), consisting mainly of Colony leadership but with a broad appeal in the Protectorate.[3] The U.P.P. had come into existence mainly as a political organization through which discontent and opposition to the establishment, particularly in the Protectorate, could be ventilated.[4] It had been formed in 1955 in an atmosphere of great political and civil unrest amounting almost to a revolt in many areas in the Protectorate against the authority of chiefs. This party had high hopes for quick political success, hopes strengthened by the knowledge of impending elections in 1957.[5] Later, in 1959, the potential of the U.P.P. was seriously weakened by a fierce and acrimonious split within the leadership and the ranks of that party. A minority then emerged as an independent political organization calling itself the Independent Progressive People's Party (I.P.P.), and sat separately in the Legislative Council under its new name.

In 1958, in the wake of a protracted struggle between Milton Margai and his younger brother, Albert, for the leadership of the S.L.P.P. after the 1957 general elections, Albert Margai left the S.L.P.P. and formed a new political party which was called the People's National Party. Prominently associated with the leadership of this party was Siaka Stevens, a former minister in the S.L.P.P. government. The P.N.P. immediately attracted most of the young intellectual and progressive elements from all sections of the country as well as those who had been uncomfortable in the S.L.P.P. with its heavy dependence on chiefs and ultraconservative policies. Many young people found in Albert Margai's leadership a happy rallying point for the forces of change and progress in the country. The P.N.P. made a dramatic impact and immediately constituted the most formidable threat the S.L.P.P. had ever had. I was one of the founding members of the P.N.P. and played a prominent role in all its activities during its rather brief existence.

Perhaps the most effective of the smaller parties during this period was the Kono Progressive Movement (K.P.M.). Formed in 1950, this party, as its name implied, was dedicated to the advancement of the interests of the people of Kono, a major tribe in the east of Sierra Leone. The Konos had a special reason for safeguarding their exclusive interests because their area was certainly the most neglected, even though, with its abundant diamonds, it contributed more than many other areas to the revenue of the country. Their community had been extensively infiltrated and eroded by diamond speculators from other parts of the country and from outside Sierra Leone. Further, they considered themselves captives of a situation from which they derived very few tangible benefits and in which they were the unfortunate victims of intolerable police supervision and provocation, due, no doubt, to the need to enforce most stringent laws designed for the protection of the diamond industry. The K.P.M., through a daring display of guts and high-powered organizational skill, completely dominated the politics of the Kono district during this period. Because of the importance of diamonds in the economy of Sierra Leone, the Government fully recognized the significance of this party's strength and the need to reach some kind of accommodation with its leaders.

In 1959, to expand its base, the Kono Progressive Movement merged with the Sierra Leone Independence Movement, a party with a strong intellectual appeal but very limited popular support, led by Dr. Edward Blyden III. The Sierra Leone Independence Movement had enjoyed for a time a refreshing and sensational impact on the politics of Sierra Leone, but soon lost its steam. This was partly because of its almost exclusively youthful intellectual appeal and partly because of its attachment to oldfangled political goals.

This strange alliance of Freetown Creole intellectuals and Kono revolutionaries, which assumed the new name of Sierra Leone Progressive Independence Movement (S.L.P.I.M.), was doomed to be short-lived. Even though it enjoyed the enthusiastic support of the Konos, it was only when it later entered an alliance with the powerful People's National Party in 1959 that the group seemed really effective. The scene was then fully set for an exciting show of strength in the months immediately preceding the Independence All Party Constitutional Conference of 1960.

The oldest of all the political parties in Sierra Leone on the eve of independence was the National Council of the Colony of Sierra Leone. Formed in 1950 as the political organ for the expression, defense, and advocacy of Creole supremacy in the political arena of Sierra Leone, it proved to be an effective opposition party which directly challenged and confronted first the British Government and later the S.L.P.P. in its claim to speak for Sierra Leone. Particularly after the publication of the constitutional proposals of 1947, the Creoles felt seriously threatened in their position of dominance in the politics of the country and in the accompanying socially superior status they affected. Under the British, the Creoles had been led to believe that as the most educated and "prepared" element in the country they were eminently most suitable to assume the responsibilities of leading Sierra Leone into independence.

The more militant and reactionary Creoles had formed themselves into the Settlers' Group. This group argued that since the Creoles were the descendants of the settlers who had been given a home in Sierra Leone after the abolition of slavery, they enjoyed certain civic and property rights and should not in any way be made to obey laws enacted by a legislature including Protectorate members whom they preferred to describe as foreigners. The Settlers' Group, even though it took the position that any elections held on the 1951 Constitution should be boycotted, preferred to assume a pseudocultural role, as the custodians of Creole culture, while most of its followers gave political support to the National Council of the Colony of Sierra Leone. The Settlers, basing their claims on constitutional rights, challenged the legality of the 1951 constitution in the Sierra Leone courts. In spite of a series of reverses in these courts, they pressed their case through appeals to the Judicial Committee of the Privy Council in the United Kingdom. For the Settlers, nothing less than the creation of the Colony area as a completely separate state was likely to be satisfactory if independence was to be given to the Protectorate as well. The Settlers, in this frame of mind, took up a most intransigent attitude and refused to be involved as a political group in any active preparations for independence. As a matter of fact, at the time of independence they had a case pending before the Privy Council in London asking for an injunction to restrain the government in Sierra Leone from putting into effect the statutory instruments for independence.

The National Council for the Colony of Sierra Leone, however, failed to make much impact in Sierra Leone outside the ranks of the extreme die-hard conservative Creoles. Most educated and progressive

Creoles, even though naturally proud of the heritage of distinguished leadership of their group, were fully aware of the realities of a new and changing Sierra Leone and of the significance of numbers in the new game of democracy which had come to stay in the country.

As if to add more color to the scene of multiple political parties in Sierra Leone during the period immediately preceding independence, the redoubtable and much-respected African nationalist figure, I. T. A. Wallace-Johnson, discontinued political affiliations with any other party and announced the establishment in 1958 of his Radical Democratic Party, with himself as its only representative in the Legislative Council. Wallace-Johnson tried to attract former members of the defunct Labor Party in the hope of crystallizing in his party the entire labor movement of the country. However, the Radical Democratic Party as a separate political organization did not last long. Wallace-Johnson soon took his party into uneasy alliance with the growingly powerful People's National Party and his group lost its identity in the larger movement, although Sierra Leone politics was to continue to hear the persistent and strident voice of Mr. Wallace-Johnson until his death.[6]

Early in 1960, following the visit to Sierra Leone of the then British Secretary of State for the Colonies, Alan Lennox-Boyd, the British Government opened secret talks for independence with the S.L.P.P.-controlled Sierra Leone Government. These secret discussions advanced to the stage at which the new constitutional proposals had reached draft form. At this juncture, Milton Margai, the S.L.P.P. leader who had become the Premier of Sierra Leone, invited all the political parties in the country to engage with the S.L.P.P. in a round-table conference in Freetown to discuss the constitutional proposals for independence. The British Government, in keeping with its policy in all such situations, had let it be known that independence would be granted only after the convening of an all-party conference in London at which discussions would be held on the details of the independence constitution and serious efforts made to reach all-party agreement on its terms.

However, the British, while recognizing the importance of achieving an all-party agreement on the crucial issue of independence, insisted that the final constitutional arrangements be regarded as an agreement between Her Majesty's Government in the United Kingdom on the one hand and the Sierra Leone Government—after all, in many

ways at that time Her Majesty's Government in Sierra Leone—on the
other. There was no doubt a good deal of wisdom in the Sierra Leone
People's Party's attitude in seeking an opportunity to iron out points
of controversy among Sierra Leonean politicians before taking the
trip to London. Indeed there were good reasons for believing that
the strong and articulate opposition parties were in a perfect position
to make the going rough at the Constitutional Independence Conference in London if some accommodations and compromises were not
reached in Freetown before the Conference. In any event, the British
must have given their blessing to this move which turned out to be
of the utmost significance in the political history of the country.

During the round table all-party pre-independence conference in
Freetown, at which I was one of the representatives of the People's
National Party, all the participant parties agreed to overlook their
political differences and, in a great show of national unity, to form
the United National Front. The avowed intention was to use their
joint efforts in the cause of independence with particular reference to
the impending Constitutional Conference and to problems thereafter
"including . . . the implementation of independence and the efficient
administration of government." [7]

To the surprise of the British public, when the Constitutional
Independence Conference was convened at Lancaster House, London,
in April 1960, across the table from the British Government side was
a united group of politicians who were determined to suspend their
feuding, close ranks, and ,achieve independence through national
unity. This situation was in marked contrast to the atmosphere that
had pervaded similar pre-independence constitutional conferences of
other British colonial territories when rival party leaders had habitually engaged in bitter exchanges in a last and determined stand to get
their own ideas for independence accepted. On such occasions the
British have often enjoyed the pleasure of holding the balance and
serving as arbitrators. In the case of Sierra Leone, presented with
the United National Front, the British had to negotiate across the
table with a unified group. In these rather unexpected circumstances,
the Sierra Leone Constitutional Independence Conference turned out
to be an exercise in mutual admiration with the British congratulating
the Sierra Leoneans and the Sierra Leoneans congratulating the
British.

Once again in the political story of Sierra Leone, one finds a most important step being taken without the fullest discussion and examination of outstanding issues. In the name of unity and the desire for the speedy achievement of independence, the leaders of the various political parties were willing to bury burning issues that had been the subject of national debate and controversy during preceding months. For example, the position of chiefs in Sierra Leone after independence had been one of the main planks of the P.N.P. platform. The National Council for the Colony of Sierra Leone had based its official position on the status of the Colony Creoles in an independent Sierra Leone. Unlike the members of the Settlers' Group—who, convinced of the justice of their claim that the Colony could not be included in an independent Sierra Leone along the lines proposed, had assumed an attitude of noncooperation—the National Council for the Colony of Sierra Leone operated within the constitutional framework and hoped to negotiate the status of Creoles within the party political system.

In the absence of extensive interparty political debate on principles and policies, it was quite clear that the creation of the United National Front was one of political convenience and not of real understanding and compromise. Milton Margai had insisted on only one condition for the union and that was that he should emerge as the leader and thus become the first Prime Minister of independent Sierra Leone. The leaders of the opposition parties had correspondingly insisted on only one condition—that they be admitted into the government immediately after the Constitutional Conference and that they continue in positions with the government after independence. For this latter concession, the leaders of the opposition parties were willing to compromise their former positions of principle on controversial matters touching the future of the nation. They were even willing to surrender their demands for elections before independence, which would have given them the chance to see their particular parties in power.

It is fair to state that when the opposition leaders thus surrendered their political positions in the cause of unity, they believed that within the framework of the United National Front it would yet be possible to hammer out compromise policies to take care of the outstanding matters of controversy. As it turned out, however, no such efforts were made when once the leaders were accepted into the government ranks either as cabinet ministers or as recipients of various forms of patronage from the government. The nation ambled along under the peaceful and benign leadership of Milton Margai, and no further debates of much moment on national questions took place.

It was left to Siaka Stevens, one of the representatives of the P.N.P.–S.L.P.I.M. coalition [8] at the Constitutional Conference, to provide the only discordant note at an otherwise very peaceful and unemotional gathering. Siaka Stevens as one of the leaders of the P.N.P. had been one of the representatives of his party at the pre-independence all-party Constitutional Conference held in Freetown. He himself had taken the most active part in all the discussions and negotiations that had preceded the establishment of the United National Front. As a matter of fact, some of the all-party caucus meetings which I attended had been held in his Freetown home and he had publicly given the most unqualified support to this coalition. When Stevens left Freetown for the London talks, we all naturally assumed that he was going to support the general position as he had not up to that time given any hint of dissentient opinion. At London's Lancaster House, Stevens waited until all the discussions had been concluded and on the final day when the British Government's official delegation was satisfied that both sides had reached agreement, chose the moment of highest drama to record his opposition. After the newsmen and television cameras had been admitted to the final session of the Conference (which up to then had been secret behind closed doors) and all the delegates were ceremoniously appending their signatures to a document they believed to be of the highest historical significance, Siaka Stevens stoutly announced, when it came to his turn, that he would not sign. He then proceeded to enumerate his reasons, the details of which he had circulated to the press beforehand. These reasons were not in any way new. They were in fact the same matters of P.N.P. policy that had been conceded by the P.N.P. when agreement was reached on the formation of a national coalition to be known as the United National Front.

In spite of the dramatics of Siaka Stevens, the independence constitution document was duly signed by all the other participants in the Conference and the terms of the agreement reached between the British Government and Sierra Leone were thereby affirmed. This document later assumed statutory authority and became the Sierra Leone Independence Constitution, 1961.

Siaka Stevens was not content to rest with his performance in London. He stormed into Freetown with much rage and fury a fortnight before the other delegates to the Conference returned. He mounted a high-geared attack on all those who had participated in the Conference, calling those who had previously belonged to opposition parties "turncoats" and representatives of the S.L.P.P. "weaklings." He proclaimed himself to be the shining courageous knight inspired by the highest patriotic zeal. There were those, however, who believed that Siaka Stevens found the courage to assume this posture because he was fully aware that he stood little chance of personally deriving much advantage from the arrangements of the United National Front. The plum of a cabinet portfolio, as he might well have seen it, was beyond his grasp as he was not at the time a member of the legislature.[9] Whatever his real motives, Siaka Stevens, after unsuccessfully challenging the leadership of Albert Margai in our own People's National Party on our return from the London Conference, announced in September, 1960, the creation of a new party under his leadership, the All People's Congress.

From its inception, the All People's Congress attracted a large following. This achievement was quite understandable given the realities of Sierra Leone politics at the time. The opposition parties for the previous few years had been working up the electorate against the Sierra Leone People's Party which had very little proper organization. The whole political climate had been conditioned for a final election effort at the polls, from which politicians had hoped to see emerge the real masters of the country to lead Sierra Leone to independence. Now they were faced with a stunning disillusionment which many regarded as a sell-out amounting to a betrayal. This was hard to refute in the face of the willingness of the leaders of the opposition parties to accept cabinet portfolios in an S.L.P.P. government that these very leaders had been holding responsible for all the ills in the country and representing as completely incapable of leadership. Besides, there were many principles that the opposition parties had cherished which were now abandoned and quite natural for the new All People's Congress to embrace. Chief of these issues was the attractive one of "elections before independence."

The All People's Congress provided a most attractive rallying platform for all types of disaffected groups. Many active politicians and their followers who saw in the United National Front a frustration of their political hopes sought solace in the A.P.C. Many Creoles who were inclined to oppose on principle any Protectorate-dominated government rushed to join the ranks of the A.P.C. to avert what they considered to be an impending national crisis if not disaster. Many Temnes and other tribal groups from the northern areas of the country, eager to destroy the hegemony of the Mendes in Sierra Leone politics, joined the A.P.C. in the hope that a non-Mende dominated party would at last come into power in the country.[10]

In these circumstances, it was not surprising that Siaka Stevens and his A.P.C. made a sensational impact on Sierra Leone politics. Only two months after the party officially came into existence, the A.P.C. easily won the elections to the Freetown City Council. Without question, the new party posed an immediate threat to the S.L.P.P. There are good reasons for believing that if Stevens and his party had succeeded in obtaining elections before independence, the All People's Congress might well have won. As it turned out, the S.L.P.P.-dominated United National Front government stoutly rejected the arguments for elections before independence.

Sierra Leone therefore achieved independence with many questions unanswered such as those relating to the role of chiefs and to uniformity of land legislation in the Colony and in the Protectorate. Owing to the creation of the United National Front, debate had subsided among the political party leaders who were now members of the S.L.P.P.-dominated government. Only the newly formed All People's Congress and the extremely conservative and reactionary Settlers' Group, for conflicting reasons, were left to express dissent. There was not even much argument or debate, since no one on the government side was listening. They had set their sights toward independence and not even a debate on fundamental national issues was likely to divert their attention. To dramatize his confidence and his new mood, a few days before independence Milton Margai clamped down on the opposition, using emergency powers to arrest leading A.P.C. politicians including Siaka Stevens and Wallace-Johnson and put them in jail where they celebrated or mourned independence.

Thus on April 27, 1961 Sierra Leone achieved independence without much national fanfare, with many questions unresolved, and with a great fund of good will and cooperation from the British. The deep and serious issues reaching the very roots of the country's problems remained to demand solution at some other day.

## NOTES

1. Dr., later Sir Milton Margai, the leader of the S.L.P.P. became the first Prime Minister of Sierra Leone.

2. Later Sir Albert Margai.

3. Prominent among other opposition parties in terms of sectional interests were the N.C.C.S.L. (National Council for the Colony of Sierra Leone) representing Colony Creole interests and the K.P.M. (Kono Progressive Movement) representing the Kono district. The Kono district has special importance as the major diamond-mining area.

4. The U.P.P. was being led by Mr. C. B. Rogers-Wright, a notorious criminal lawyer (later disbarred in a case presided over by the then Chief Justice Bairamian) who also specialized in flamboyant and dishonest practices to gain court victories. Wright was able to use the riots and disturbances in the Protectorate in 1955 for political advantage and his party, the U.P.P., provided a rallying platform for all dissent and opposition.

5. As it turned out the S.L.P.P. won the 1957 elections handsomely with an impressive majority.

6. Wallace-Johnson, who died in Accra, Ghana, in 1965 while attending an Afro-Asian solidarity conference, had been for nearly four decades in the vanguard of African nationalist movements. In the 1930s he led nationalist movements first in Ghana later in his native Sierra Leone, where he is revered as one of the earliest and most effective nationalist leaders.

7. Sierra Leone *Daily Mail,* March 28, 1960.

8. The P.N.P.–S.L.P.I.M. coalition was represented at the Conference by Albert Margai (later Prime Minister), Siaka Stevens (who was later A.P.C. leader and also Prime Minister), Tamba Mbriwa (leader of the former Kono Progressive Movement who later became a Paramount Chief in the Kono district), and Gershon Collier (the author, then a practicing lawyer and constitutional-legal adviser of the P.N.P. who became Secretary-General of the United National Front and at independence was appointed Permanent Representative to the U.N.).

9. Siaka Stevens, even though he had won the seat for Port Loko East in the last general elections (1957) had been unseated as the result of a successful election petition brought against him. Under the Sierra Leone Constitution, only members of Parliament could hold a cabinet portfolio.

10. Siaka Stevens, the A.P.C. leader, is generally reported as belonging to the Limba tribe from the northern province. Other northern tribal groups sympathetic to the A.P.C. include the Susus, Lokkos, and Mandingos.

# CHAPTER 4

# The Constitution of Independence, 1961

Since the inception of the Colony, the British had habitually introduced written constitutions in Sierra Leone, as indeed they did in all their territories even though the British themselves do not possess one. They depend on conventions sanctified by centuries of use to guide the government of the state. The British, however, consider it necessary to give newly independent states written constitutions since many of these states have not had the centuries of experience that would permit them to exist without such a safeguard.

The Sierra Leone Independence Constitution, following the Indian, Nigerian, and other Commonwealth experiences, is a document which dealt not only with purely constitutional matters, but also with guarantees pertaining to fundamental human rights and freedoms for the individual within the state. Even though it does not appear that English constitutional lawyers favor the inclusion of such guarantees in constitutional instruments, the British Government has inscribed in every independence constitution given to their former Asian and African colonial territories a chapter on fundamental rights.[1]

In the Sierra Leone Independence Constitution the sections relating to fundamental rights were included in what are known as Entrenched Clauses. These clauses require a special procedure for amendment to ensure the protection of the individual within the state, and to safeguard minority and special interest groups.[2]

The Independence Constitution of 1961 was in many ways modeled on the Nigerian Independence Constitution of 1960. In other ways it preserved the essential approach of the Sierra Leone Constitutions of 1924 and 1951. In every way it was a product of British constitutional ideas drawn from the British experience, both in the area of statutory provisions and in the area of conventions.

The first chapter of the Constitution quite properly deals with the subject of citizenship. An important feature of the type of artificial nationhood that colonialism created was the dubious status of the citizens of such states. Sierra Leone, like most colonial territories, was created without any consideration for ethnic or linguistic realities, and was defined only geographically in terms of settled boundaries. Since Sierra Leone as a country did not come into existence until 1808, it was important that, at the advent of independence, the definition of a Sierra Leonean should be spelled out.

Prior to independence, all Sierra Leoneans were either British subjects or British-protected persons. Those who were born in the Colony automatically became British subjects and enjoyed all the legal and constitutional privileges of British subjects, which meant that their legal rights were exactly similar to those enjoyed by British persons born in the United Kingdom or in other parts of the British Commonwealth. On the other hand, those who were born in the Protectorate were legally aliens and technically did not owe any allegiance to the British Crown.[3] They merely enjoyed "protection" from the British Crown and thus distinctly belonged to a different category of citizenship. It was only proper that at independence the anomaly of Sierra Leoneans, within the same country, belonging to two different categories of citizenship should be corrected and uniformity of status achieved. Unfortunately, the logic of uniformity, which was properly applied to the matter of citizenship, was not pursued in any similar manner in other controversial questions such as the laws affecting title and ownership of land in the Colony and in the Protectorate. After all, the whole idea of independence was to create a new nation in Sierra Leone, obliterating for good all differences and anomalies inherent in the concepts of a Colony and a Protectorate.

The Independence Constitution still preserved the idea of the sovereignty of the Queen of England. The section relating to Parliament clearly states that "Parliament . . . shall consist of Her Majesty and a House of Representatives." [4] This concept of the Queen of England as head of the government of Sierra Leone and the embodiment of the sovereignty of the country is founded on British constitutional principles. Sovereignty resides in the Queen as supreme head of government and the government is actually administered by her ministers on her behalf. This doctrine is quite easy to understand within the context of territorial Britain; but it is another matter when it is extended to her "realms beyond the seas" especially when such "realms" are in Asia and Africa. The doctrine is, in fact, part of the general idea of the British Commonwealth. Sierra Leone undertook to accept this relationship after independence as an important part of the details agreed to in the London pre-independence Constitutional Conference in 1960.

As Sierra Leone thus became a member-state of the British Commonwealth, the Head of State under the Constitution continued to be the Queen of England in whom executive authority was vested. The representative of the Queen in Sierra Leone on whose behalf the executive authority is exercisable is her appointee, the Governor-General. The relevant section in the Constitution states:

> There shall be a Governor-General and Commander-in-Chief of Sierra Leone, who shall be appointed by Her Majesty and shall hold office during Her Majesty's pleasure and who shall be Her Majesty's representative in Sierra Leone.[5]

Even though the Queen makes the appointment, she does so only on the advice of the Prime Minister and government in Sierra Leone. Sir Maurice Dorman, the last colonial governor before independence became the first Governor-General after independence. In 1962, Sir Henry Lightfoot-Boston, a Sierra Leonean, became Governor-General succeeding Sir Maurice Dorman.

This executive authority of the Queen exists in theory only. In practice, the Prime Minister and his cabinet in Sierra Leone have supreme authority and give advice to the Governor-General which he is obliged invariably to accept. In fact, the Governor-General automatically has to accept the advice of the government in all matters, particularly in the appointment as Prime Minister of someone he believes likely to command majority support in Parliament.[6]

All legislation, to be effective, has to be passed by the House of Representatives and signed by the Governor-General on behalf of the Queen. An interesting feature of the Sierra Leone Independence Constitution is the absence of a second or upper chamber. This is distinctly different from the United Kingdom constitutional practice, from which so much else has been copied into the Constitution; and it also differs from the pattern in India and Nigeria.

The Sierra Leone House of Representatives comprises a Speaker and two categories of members of Parliament—Chief members and ordinary members. Twelve Paramount Chiefs are elected from each of the twelve administrative districts in the former Sierra Leone Protectorate—not by the general electorate of these districts, but by tribal authorities. For this purpose constituencies are determined and the total number of such members may be prescribed by Parliament.[7]

Thus members of the House of Representatives (Parliament), are elected by two different methods—the Paramount Chiefs, indirectly, and the ordinary members, directly. This dual method of election has created a situation in which some persons in the former Protectorate enjoy double representation and can therefore vote twice—that is if such persons are also tribal authorities. Since the constituencies of Paramount Chiefs and ordinary members holding Protectorate seats are the same and they overlap.

Even though different methods of election are used, there is nothing in the Constitution to suggest any difference in the rights enjoyed when once the members have been elected and taken their seats in Parliament. It is, for example, constitutionally possible for any of the Paramount Chiefs to be appointed Prime Minister; and there is nothing to debar any Paramount Chief from being appointed a minister and to serve in the cabinet as indeed many of them have done.

When once the Prime Minister has been appointed by the Governor-General, he has to win a vote of confidence in Parliament to demonstrate his ability to command majority support of the members. Within this framework, the party system operates and the leader of the party with a majority during the life of that Parliament remains Prime Minister as long as he is able to maintain such majority support.

In the Independence Constitution, Parliament emerges as the supreme law-making body entrusted "to make laws for the peace, order, and good government of Sierra Leone." [8] This authority is limited only in the case of the entrenched clauses previously mentioned. These are clauses in the Constitution that cannot be altered by a bill passed by a simple majority in the House of Representatives as is the case with all other clauses not so described. A bill to alter any of the entrenched clauses, as set out in Section 43 of the 1961 Sierra Leone Constitution, "shall not be submitted to the Governor-General for his assent unless the bill has been passed by the House of Representatives in two successive sessions, there having been a dissolution of Parliament between the first and second of those sessions." [9]

The idea of "entrenched clauses" is crucial to the Constitution because it protects certain important provisions from easy amendment by a Parliament which might not at that particular time be truly representative of the majority of the people even though the government might have a narrow majority in the House of Representatives. By the requirement that such a bill may be submitted to the Governor-General only after passage by the House of Representatives in two successive sessions, with a dissolution and general elections intervening, the people are given a chance to pronounce on the particular issue directly through such a general election. After this consultation with the people, so to speak, the members of Parliament can then feel mandated to proceed with passage of the particular bill.

The entrenched clauses cover important questions like the status of the Queen of England and Parliament within the Constitution. They also protect the institution of Paramount Chieftaincy, and cover the status of the Judiciary, certain public officials, the Director of Audit, and the Public Service Commission.

The most important sections of the Constitution included in the entrenched clauses are those relating to "Fundamental Human Rights." [10] During the hundred and fifty years or so that the British were in control in Sierra Leone, the rights of the individual within the state were well respected and protected. The British gave to their colonies British concepts not only of government and administration but of law and justice. As a matter of fact, the fundamental rights that were included in the Constitution as entrenched clauses were in essence a consolidation of accepted concepts of law and justice derived from the English common law; in some cases they were mere adaptations of provisions already contained in Sierra Leone Statutes. Even in Sierra Leone tribal life, human rights have always been protected, though not to the same extent as under British rule.[11]

In spite of the fact that the concept of fundamental rights was not new to Sierra Leone, it was considered necessary and important that they not only be included in the constitution, but entrenched. There were various reasons for this. Chief among them was the tribal and minority issue. Because of the circumstances surrounding the establishment of Sierra Leone as a nation, the country at independence comprised many different tribal and ethnic groups. These groups had many distinctive practices and customs which might well have suffered had an arrogant majority taken control and chosen to trample on special tribal interests and individual rights.

Sierra Leone is a country of at least thirteen major tribes, speaking different languages and often having different religious and social customs. There were also living in Sierra Leone at the time of independence sizable groups of Asians and Europeans belonging to different races and cultural backgrounds. Under British rule all groups were able to live together in Sierra Leone and enjoy direct protection from the British presence whose authority was easily enforceable. Now that independence was imminent, real fears were expressed by some minority groups, notably the Settlers that their special interests would be in jeopardy after independence. The inclusion of these clauses was largely to allay such fears.

There was also, of course, the burning issue between the Colony and the Protectorate and this too was of a tribal nature. The Creoles of the Colony, particularly those of the Settlers' Group, had posed important questions relating to what they described as special interests derived by virtue of their ancestors having been the pioneer settlers. In answer to these questions, the British assured them that through the entrenchment of fundamental human rights in the Constitution their special interests would be protected. In this way, the British sought to assure the Creole minority that their vital interests would not suffer at the hands of a Protectorate majority in Parliament.

As with the Creoles, so it was with other minority tribes at the time of independence. They were all made to believe that through the entrenchment of fundamental rights in the Constitution their special interests would be protected and they would enjoy the essential freedoms under the law. Further, the existence of entrenched clauses in independence constitutions of postcolonial territories like Sierra Leone was meant to prove to the international community that these "primitive" countries were no longer savage and uncivilized, but were ready to conform to universal norms of civilized behavior. The British were quite determined to demonstrate on record that the newly independent nation fulfilled international qualifications for independence and was ready to conform to internationally approved concepts of human rights as set out in the Convention on Human Rights to which the British had adhered on behalf of their colonies. Examples of entrenched clauses are those relating to protection from slavery and forced labor,[12] and protection from inhuman treatment.[13]

All the sections relating to fundamental rights and individual freedoms are entrenched in the Constitution.[14] They could be divided roughly under three heads: first, those concerned with the freedom of the individual within the state. In this category are those which relate to protection of the right of life,[15] protection of the individual from arbitrary arrest or detention,[16] protection of the individual's freedom of movement,[17] and protection from slavery and forced labor.[18] Second, those concerned with protection of property rights. In this category are those which relate to protection from deprivation of property [19] and protection for privacy of home and other property.[20] Finally, those concerned with general fundamental rights. In this category are guarantees of the protection of law, including due process, and the authority of the courts; [21] of freedom of conscience; [22] freedom of expression; [23] of freedom of assembly and association,[24] and protection from discrimination on the grounds of race or any other ground.[25]

It is doubtful how effective written enactments in constitutions can be. The experience of European states formed after the war, in whose constitutions similar provisions have been inserted, has not been particularly encouraging. Some distinguished British jurists believe such abstract declarations are useless unless there exist the will and the means to make them effective.[26] The British Government was fully aware of the difficulties of enforcing and sometimes interpreting such provisions.[27] Yet, in spite of these considerations, the British thought it necessary to insist that these clauses be inserted in the Independence Constitution.

The Sierra Leone Independence Constitution, 1961, was clearly meant to be a blueprint for the future of Sierra Leone. It was based on the application of Western democratic principles of government closely following the British pattern.

In some sections, such as those relating to chieftaincy, the Independence Constitution sought to preserve indigenous ideas of government and entrenched tribal institutions in an otherwise completely

British-style constitution.[28] The wisdom of this development is doubtful since no serious attempt had previously been made to democratize these institutions, notably chieftaincy, before thus including them in a constitutional system based on Western ideas of democracy. The British, who had been so careful to protect and preserve tribal customs and practice during the nearly seventy years of their control over that part of the country, were now quite ready almost overnight to expose the people of the Protectorate to a parliamentary system quite alien to their experience.

It should be recalled that the first modern Sierra Leone Constitution of 1924 had been introduced to satisfy the political aspirations of the Creole community in the Colony. These Creoles, because of their background and experience, had been able to completely accept British ideas of government to which they had already been accustomed, and they had been electing their representatives ever since that time. The Protectorate, on the other hand, had been represented in the Legislative Council under the 1924 Constitution only by nominated members, that is by appointees of the colonial government—a clear departure from Western-style democratic practice. Even under the 1951 constitution, the last constitution implemented before the 1961 Independence Constitution was introduced, the Protectorate had been represented in the Legislative Council by members who had been indirectly elected. This method of election is distinctly different from the Western-style democratic election provided for in the Colony under that Constitution.

Now upon achieving independence, Sierra Leone, comprising the former Colony and the former Protectorate, attempted to operate on a constitution erected on these shaky foundations. It was not surprising that such an experiment in democracy, with this constitution as its blueprint, was doomed to failure from the start. Six short years after independence the whole structure collapsed following a disputed election. In the face of national chaos the military took over, dismissed the Governor-General, revoked the constitution, and embarked on illegal, authoritarian rule. Fortunately, however, a year later, after yet another military coup, civilian rule was restored and the constitution re-instated.

## NOTES

1. Godfrey K. J. Amachree, *Howard Law Journal,* Vol. 2, 1965. "Human Rights in Nigeria."
2. Sierra Leone Independence Constitution, 1961, Sec. 43 (b).
3. Foreign Jurisdiction Act, 1890.
4. Constitution of Sierra Leone, 1961, Ch. IV, Sec. 29.
5. Constitution of Sierra Leone, 1961, Ch. III, Sec. 26.
6. Constitution of Sierra Leone, Sec. 58 (2) and Sec. 64 (1) and Sec. 57.
7. Constitution of Sierra Leone, 1961, Sec. 30 (a) and (b).
8. Constitution of Sierra Leone, 1961, Sec. 42.
9. Constitution of Sierra Leone, 1961, Sec. 43 (1) (a), (b), (c), and (d).
10. Constitution of Sierra Leone, 1961, Secs. 11–25.
11. Kenneth L. Little, *The Mende of Sierra Leone,* p. 175.
12. Constitution of Sierra Leone, 1961, Sec. 15.
13. Constitution of Sierra Leone, 1961, Sec. 16.
14. Constitution of Sierra Leone, 1961, Ch. II, Secs. 11–25.
15. Constitution of Sierra Leone, 1961, Ch. II, Sec. 12.
16. Constitution of Sierra Leone, 1961, Sec. 13.
17. Constitution of Sierra Leone, 1961, Sec. 14.
18. Constitution of Sierra Leone, 1961, Sec. 15.
19. Constitution of Sierra Leone, 1961, Sec. 17.
20. Constitution of Sierra Leone, 1961, Sec. 18.
21. Constitution of Sierra Leone, 1961, Sec. 19.
22. Constitution of Sierra Leone, 1961, Sec. 20.
23. Constitution of Sierra Leone, 1961, Sec. 21.
24. Constitution of Sierra Leone, 1961, Sec. 22.
25. Constitution of Sierra Leone, 1961, Sec. 23.
26. Report of Simon Commission on the Indian Constitution. Also see Jennings, *Some Characteristics of the Indian Constitution* (1953), pp. 3–4, 48, 54, Jennings, *The Approach to Self Government* (1956), pp. 100, 110, and Wheare, *Modern Constitutions* (1951), p. 17.
27. Report of Commission on Nigerian Independence Constitution, p. 97, par. 38.
28. Sierra Leone Independence Constitution, 1961, Sec. 44.

# CHAPTER 5

# The Colony-Protectorate Problem

Prominent among the problems which have always dominated Sierra Leone politics is one generally described as the Colony-Protectorate issue, which to be understood requires expanded definition of the Colony and the Protectorate.

The Colony consisted roughly of the peninsula area, southern Koya, and the Sherbro District, including the outlying islands of Bonthe. This area included land originally acquired from the Temnes for the first settlement and later transferred by the Sierra Leone Company to the British Crown, as well as additional land acquired by cession, annexation, and treaty from 1807 on. The Protectorate comprised the rest of the country in the hinterland which came under British protection in 1896 and was described at the time, as "foreign countries adjoining the Colony," and "territories lying on the British side of the French and Liberian frontiers." [1]

The Colony area was first acquired to provide a home on the continent of Africa for natives of Africa and their descendants who had become displaced persons for various reasons, but mainly because of the abolition of slavery and the slave trade.

The first settlement in 1787 was made by a group known as the Black Poor. It consisted of some five hundred persons, mainly destitute black emancipated slaves, who had taken refuge in London and other large English cities following the judgment of Lord Mansfield in 1772 which had the effect of immediate freedom for any slave setting foot on English soil.[2] The settlement was doomed to failure as climatic conditions, the temperamental unsuitability of the settlers, and the unfriendliness of the neighboring Temnes conspired to frustrate the hopes of the founding fathers. However, after the burning of Granville Town, as the first settlement was called, other settlers arrived.[3]

The next important group came in 1792. These were known as Nova Scotians. They were former slaves from the United States who had fought in the American War of Independence on the side of the British and had been settled after the War as free men or as servants of Loyalists in Nova Scotia, Canada.[4]

After the Nova Scotians, another group known as the Maroons arrived in 1800. The Maroons were recaptured slaves with a reputation for very warlike behavior who had been settled in Nova Scotia after successfully revolting against their British masters in Jamaica.[5]

These three groups—the Granville Town original settlers, the Nova Scotians, and the Maroons—soon formed a distinct community in Sierra Leone which was neither wholly European nor wholly African. They were detribalized Africans who had lost their African cultural heritage through many years of living in an alien situation. Most of them, like their fathers before them, had been born in America and Europe. Many had never previously lived in Africa and were complete strangers to African tribal life. They spoke no African language but used instead a form of patois composed predominantly of English words. They aped Western values and patterns of behavior as they had seen them while in the service of their slave-masters in Western countries. In many cases, their affectations in dress, manners, and speech were ludicrous caricatures of Western values and behavior patterns since in many details their African origins were in fact quite apparent. Yet they were sufficiently different from the surrounding indigenous tribes who had never been taken into slavery to enable them later to persuade themselves that they belonged to a superior class.

Into this cultural atmosphere came the "Liberated Africans," a still later group of settlers, and it was this value standard that they also soon accepted and emulated. The Liberated Africans were slaves who had been captured on the high seas from slave ships on their way to America. Following the passing in England in 1807 of the Slave Trade Act, a court of adjudicature called the court of Vice-Admiralty was set up in Sierra Leone for trial of the masters of slave ships and the release of slaves.[6] For the next fifty years and more, a steady stream of liberated slaves flowed into the expanding community of settlers in Sierra Leone. These tribal Africans spoke their several languages and practised their various tribal customs. At first they were treated with contempt by the earlier settlers. Soon, however, after the Liberated Africans had distinguished themselves in business and other spheres of life, they were integrated into a homogeneous class of nonindigenous Sierra Leoneans who became known as Creoles. The name *Creole* has since been used to describe the descendants of all the various groups of settlers including Liberated Africans who came to make their home in the Colony of Sierra Leone. In time, Creoles were distinguished from other Sierra Leoneans as those born in the Colony whose ancestors belonged to one or other of the groups of settlers with nonindigenous Sierra Leonean tribal background.

The Creoles assumed characteristics all their own and regarded themselves as a distinctive class. They believed themselves to be like the ancient children of Israel—a people apart with a special destiny who had at last arrived in their "promised land." With their experience of life in the Western world and their deep devotion to Christianity, they saw themselves as not only different from the indigenous tribes around but distinctly superior. Unlike their tribal neighbors, they were ardent practitioners of the Western culture and civilization which their British colonial masters had held up as the standard for all men. This Creole group soon constituted an elite class, first of traders and merchants, later of lawyers, doctors, teachers, journalists, and clergymen. They enjoyed higher education than the indigenous Sierra Leoneans and a reasonably high standard of living. They soon became the civil servants entrusted with great responsibilities, and their energies and intelligence ran the civil service machine in Sierra Leone.

In the service of Christianity they soon became priests, teachers, and missionaries and did much to spread their religion, education, and trade into the hinterland. The Creoles were well steeped in the Christian way of living, to which they paid ostentatious homage. The founding fathers of the Colony had sought to produce on African soil a Christian community guided by democratic institutions of government. The Creoles readily grasped educational opportunities and before long they became easily comparable in their piety and their learning to similar groups of Christians in Europe.

The Creoles also took to trade and the learned professions and distinguished themselves most remarkably. In their personal lives they aspired to European bourgeois standards, with their dinners, balls, fairs, and horse races. In their cultural lives, with amateur theatricals and literary, religious, scientific, and philosophic societies, they demonstrated the extent to which they had successfully imbibed western European value standards. The majority were self-centered, property-owning individuals, fully aware of their civil and property rights. With the assimilation of some of the finest values from western European civilization came also the inculcation in the Colony Creole society of some of the worst excesses and by-products of that civilization, as exemplified by the Europeans who lived among them. Yet the Creoles preserved a certain number of customs indigenous to their various tribes of origin, generously flavored by their newly acquired "Western civilized" living. Side by side with their ostentatious Christianity, they practised tribal rites and gaily indulged in ancestral customs which often conflicted with orthodox Christianity.

The social and cultural life in the Colony had a distinction and flavor all its own. The independence of the Creole women, for example, had no parallel either in European or African tribal life. Derived no doubt from their background in slavery, the Creole women demonstrated independence of their men by operating as petty traders both in the Colony and in the Protectorate. Some owned their own factories and ventured to trade as far afield as the Gambia. Marriage ties did not appear to have inhibited them in their purusit of success in commerce. The Creole men enjoyed a certain freedom unknown to either Europeans or tribal Africans in their relations with women and children outside institutional marriage relationships. In all they did, the Creoles struggled to preserve a separate culture from that of the Protectorate tribes and preferred to identify their African origins with the West Indies, Ghana, Nigeria, and other parts of West Africa rather than with the Protectorate hinterland.

The land on which the original settlement was established had belonged to the Temne tribe. Negotiations for its acquisition had been conducted by the sub-King Tom on behalf of the powerful Temne King Naimbana whose headquarters were up the Sierra Leone River at Robana and Robaga.[7] These Temnes had been accustomed to meeting and trading with Europeans and other foreign groups. But when they had to live in close contact with an alien settlement comprising people affecting different manners, speaking another language, and dressing very strangely, they found the experience very trying indeed.

After the establishment of the Colony, the Creole settlers of necessity had constant contacts first with the Temnes and later with the other indigenous tribes of the country. The encounter in those early days was not always friendly. As a matter of fact, twice during this period, the Temnes burned the town down. In those days, the Temne chiefs did not hesitate to wreak vengeance on the settlers when they considered it necessary.[8]

Right from the start, from the days of Dala Modu, a Mandinka trader who settled with his clan in the Colony toward the end of the eighteenth century, some people of the hinterland made their home among the Creoles and practised their tribal customs within the Colony. Indigenous tribesmen during those days came to work as laborers in the Colony and their children worked as servants in the homes of Europeans and Settlers. Even the children of chiefs were often sent down to Freetown for education and citizens of the Colony, including some in the highest positions, acted as their patrons.[9] It was not long before tribal peoples from the hinterland began intermarrying with Colony Creoles. Besides those who settled in the Colony, hundreds more came in for months at a time to provide migrant labor in the plantations, industries, and farms of the Colony. Madinka and Fula traders, Bulom and Temne laborers and artisans came by the hundreds to swell the Colony population and to add their own distinctive color to the Freetown scene.

In spite of this seemingly friendly relationship between the peoples of the Colony and the hinterland, the Temnes never really forgot that the land which served as the Colony settlement originally belonged to them. This feeling was aggravated by the expansionist policies of the British operating from the Colony. By 1807, the original Colony area had been considerably extended westwards by conquests to include almost the whole of the peninsula. This policy was not restricted to conquest and cession; it also included trade. By the turn of the eighteenth century, scores of Colony settlers had moved into the hinterland to make permanent homes there in pursuit of trade. Religion was another consideration which sent the early Creoles into the hinterland. Extremely zealous in their Christianity, the Colony Creoles felt they had a civilizing and Christianizing mission to fulfill among the hinterland tribes.

In these twin objectives of trade and religion, the Creoles had ready allies in the British and other Europeans operating from the Colony. After all, Granville Sharp had succeeded in floating the Sierra Leone Company for the establishment of the Colony only by emphasizing the commercial possibilities of the settlement.[10] Europeans were already aware of the great opportunities trade offered in the interior of Africa. Unfortunately, trade in those days still included the slave trade, an activity in which regrettably some settlers from the Colony also engaged.[11]

The Colony Creoles at first served as agents of European traders and adventurers based in the Colony. Without capital of their own, the Creoles in this way were able to penetrate into the hinterland and to exploit trading opportunities. Before long, they established flourishing businesses of their own in the hinterland. In their own boats, they plied the Sierra Leone rivers right into the heart of the hinterland.

With the expansion of trade into the hinterland, came the realization of the importance of law and order in those areas. This led to the adoption by the British of a policy of interference in the tribal wars of the neighboring tribes in the hinterland with the avowed intent of preserving the peace. In this undertaking, the services of the Colony Creoles were enlisted. The policy soon led to annexations and to blatant and high-handed interference in tribal affairs by British colonial authorities to protect trading and proprietary interests.[12] The traders also interfered with impunity and were always able to count on British official support in these adventures. Whenever the people attempted resistance, massive military intervention was used to bully and terrorize them into submission.

The chiefs of the tribes naturally resented a situation which permitted British subjects to commit outrages in their territories with impunity. They were unable to appreciate the legal nicety which restricted the punishment of crimes by British subjects to those committed within a British jurisdiction, which did not then include the hinterland. An attempt was made to improve the situation by introducing into treaties made with chiefs after 1851 the concept of the cession of Crown jurisdiction over British subjects exercisable under the Foreign Jurisdiction Act of 1843.[13] This proved inadequate to check the excesses outside the law which Colony traders could still perpetrate beyond Colony boundaries. An Imperial Act was therefore passed in 1861 making British subjects liable to punishment under

English law for offences committed "from the Rio Grande to the Gallinas and 500 miles eastwards." [14] These pieces of legislation, however, still did not completely take care of the legal problems raised by Colony and European traders' penetration of the interior. As Colony citizens and as British subjects, they were still exposed to molestations and outrages which their own conduct often provoked. A British act was passed in 1871 to cope with some of the problems thus created, which extended the jurisdiction of the Supreme Court over "crimes committed by British subjects" or "by persons not subjects of any civilized power within twenty miles of the boundaries of the West African settlement." [15]

In 1888, to enhance further the trading conditions in the rest of the country for traders from the Colony, detailed plans were drawn up and adopted for laying out a chain of roads connecting the river heads and for forming a frontier thirty miles inland to be patrolled by paramilitary police. The motivation for these plans was partly to ensure the protection of Colony citizens when they ventured into the hinterland, and partly to promote the policy of expansion which the government in Freetown seemed at this time to have adopted. It was no longer enough for the Colony-based government to make occasional forays into the interior to influence the course of events there. It was now considered important that a permanent British presence should be established in the hinterland for the protection of Colony interests. The tribal peoples had clearly demonstrated their capacity to inflict humiliating defeats on ill-prepared military expeditions from the Colony.[16]

The British colonial authorities felt by this time that the interference and infiltration from the Colony was such as to pose a real problem for the preservation of law and order in the interior area unless something positive was done to bring the situation under control. As a policy of withdrawal was considered unthinkable, the only alternative, as they saw it, was complete involvement.

The British then began persuading the chiefs to build roads and to accept the presence of police from the Colony in their districts. The presence of the police was explained as necessary for the protection of the chiefs, presumably from other chiefs and from Colony traders. The chiefs were assured that there would be no interference in their government nor would there by any interference in their "domestic institutions." "Domestic institutions" in this context included tribal institutions and perhaps slavery! [17] No doubts were left in the minds of the Sierra Leonean peoples, however, that this new policy included an element of coercion and that the police intended to keep peace through the unrestricted use of whatever force and brutality they considered necessary. The chiefs appear to have acquiesced in this new policy of protection—a policy which included road building, policing tribal districts, and the assumption of responsibility for the preservation of law and order.[18]

In 1890, an ordinance was passed which formally established the police force that was to serve as the instrument of British presence in the country outside of the Colony. This body, known as the Frontier Police, was a paramilitary force meant for the subjugation of the tribes. It was officered by Europeans and Creoles. The lower ranks were staffed by recruits from almost every tribe, as their knowledge of the languages was invaluable for their role as advisers to the chiefs. If the Creole traders expected the establishment of the Frontier Police to constitute an answer to their prayers for the immediate annexation of the interior and the protection for their interests there, however, they were disappointed. The British declined to provide the Creoles with special protection or any protection whatever in their transactions in the hinterland. The British Government's practice, in spite of some legislation to the contrary, was not to accept any obligation to protect Creoles or Europeans beyond the Colony jurisdiction. They took care to explain that the Frontier Police had no authority to interfere with the rule of chiefs. At this stage, even though there was no formal assumption of British jurisdiction over the area, colonial officials never hesitated to interfere in tribal affairs when they considered it to be in keeping with British interests to do so.

By a unilateral act of the British Government, the hinterland was annexed and proclaimed as the Sierra Leone Protectorate in August, 1896.[19] This action was at the time justified as "being best for the interests of the people." [20] By an Order in Council declaring that the Crown had acquired jurisdiction in foreign countries adjoining the Colony, the Protectorate and the Colony came to be governed by the British as one territory.

From the beginning, the British set up two separate systems of government—one in the Colony, and one in the Protectorate. In the Colony, the constitution of 1863 with its provisions for Legislative and

Executive Councils wore the trappings of democratic institutions having a semblance of limited representation by the people. The people of the Colony understood this system of government since their previous cultural experiences had prepared them for it. In the Colony villages the Creoles had virtually been governing themselves through democratic institutions with little outside supervision even before the 1863 Constitution. The people of the Protectorate, on the other hand, even though their tribal institutions including chieftaincy had strong suggestions of democracy, were more familiar with a hereditary system which preserved the authoritarian rule of the chief.

At the time of annexation, the Protectorate comprised many tribes indigenously African. Despite many centuries of contacts with Europeans and the outside world, the Protectorate tribes regarded Europeans as aliens and saw no reason why they should emulate their way of life. These tribes had their customs of which they were extremely proud, and were perfectly able to govern themselves as they had, in fact, done for centuries. The intertribal wars with which they were incessantly engaged were regarded as a way of life and necessary for the survival of the group. They understood only one method by which a group could be subjugated by another and that was by military conquest. They lived in small closely knit communities without feeling the necessity for a central powerful government except in those cases where they were aware of their duty to a powerful king or warrior who could make claim to their military services when the occasion demanded. Slavery was institutionalized as a humane social system necessary to provide the labor required for their agricultural economy. Thus warfare and slavery, the latter often providing adequate justification for the former, constituted the main foundations of Protectorate life.

For livelihood they were content to rely on agriculture which easily flourished in a land blessed with abundant rainfall, plenty of sunshine, and a rich soil. Agriculture was supplemented by hunting, fishing, and weaving. Unlike the Colony Creoles, who paid homage to respectability by upholding monogamy, the Protectorate peoples freely and honestly recognized polygamy as a social institution. Unlike the Colony inhabitants, who had been predominantly influenced by Christianity, the tribes of the Protectorate were greatly influenced by Islam as well as by Christianity. Muslim missionaries and traders had for centuries penetrated this area and through the years links had been established with North Africa and the interior of the continent, thereby preserving contacts with the glorious civilizations of Timbuktu and Africa's great historic past. These contacts had produced in the Protectorate tribes a confidence and dignity far removed from the humiliations and complexes that slavery inflicted on its victims. The spread of Islam in the Protectorate had been accomplished largely through the exploits of the invading Muslim Mandinkas and Fulas.

Many early European observers spoke approvingly of the innate superiority of the deportment and culture of the tribal Africans in the Protectorate area, in contrast with the Creoles of the Colony who had been corrupted and contaminated by contacts with Europeans. In fact, it seems to have been generally agreed during this period by objective observers that Africans were more civilized the further they were from the coast. The sophistication and polish of the Muslim Africans from the hinterland of Sierra Leone, free from the corruption, hypocrisy, and inconsistencies of the Europeans in Freetown went a long way to justify this opinion.[21] In their early contacts with the Europeans and Creoles in the Protectorate area, the Protectorate chiefs regarded them as settlers on sufferance. They were tolerated only because the tribal chiefs found them useful for the ammunition their trade provided for warfare, and the rum, tobacco, and gin such trade furnished for their pleasures. They regarded the missionaries as harmless eccentrics who gave them sufficient education to enable them to secure better bargains in their transactions with traders and British officials. Unlike the Colony Creoles, the people of the Protectorate looked askance at European customs as distinctly alien and inferior, to be utilized only for the sake of practical benefits. For example, it was considered strictly against proper etiquette for a chief to speak English in the presence of his people.[22]

In the many years of contact with Europeans, the peoples of the Protectorate, led by their chiefs, never regarded themselves as inferior nor of subservient status. When they were approached by British officials from the Colony on any transaction it was considered that a favor was being sought. They knew the land belonged to them and they had their own ideas of law and government—ideas that had been sanctified by years of experience and use. True, the chiefs appeared willing enough to accept the establishment of the Sierra Leone Protectorate, but subsequent events of the Hut Tax War clearly showed that they had believed themselves to be merely acknowledging the paternal interests of a powerful neighbor without implying any subordination.

When the British came to annex the Protectorate, they were fully aware of many distinguishing features in the lives of its peoples. They therefore decided to rule as far as possible through the tribal leaders, adopting the policy of Indirect Rule which had been satisfactorily implemented in other parts of Africa. This policy called for a recognition of tribal customs and of the authority of tribal laws. It was generally agreed that it was unwise to submit people so suddenly to a strange system of government.

Perhaps the most noticeable differences within the system introduced by the British were in the field of law. In the Colony, the English common law prevailed and the jurisdiction of the courts was completely patterned after the British system. Statutes passed in Britain up to 1880 were enforced even in the Sierra Leone courts. The right of trial by jury was enjoyed by the citizens of the Colony, though in civil cases it was later withdrawn. In the Protectorate, the jurisdiction of English law was limited to certain serious criminal cases. The District Commissioner, sitting as a magistrate in the Protectorate, was guided but not bound by English legal procedure. Even though the British had stated at the time of annexation that domestic institutions in the Protectorate would not be interfered with, a rival system of law was imposed through the use of District Commissioners which tended to supersede tribal laws in cases of conflict.

The annexation of the Sierra Leone Protectorate cast together the fortunes of the peoples of the Colony and the adjoining area. Though both groups were Africans and all more or less tribal in origin, because of their different cultural and educational experiences and the operation of British colonial policy, serious difficulties marred the relationship of the two groups.

British policy at first seemed to have been in favor of the Colony Creoles. Almost all the institutions of secondary and higher education were in Freetown. The Creoles, because of their superior education, were the civil servants and the administrators who enjoyed the maximum benefits from British presence in the country, but this also marked them in the eyes of the Protectorate people as the agents and collaborators of the British. The Creoles were the beneficiaries of Christian missionary effort in the country and they responded satisfactorily to the educational and civilizing efforts lavished on them.

No wonder that when the Protectorate rose in 1898 in bloody rebellion against the British and all they stood for, the Creoles, though Africans, were not spared but perished with the Europeans in the holocaust.

From their earliest contacts, there was not much love lost between the Creoles of the Colony and the indigenous tribes of the Protectorate. The Creoles with their superior airs and European affectations felt little sympathy for the people they sneeringly and patronizingly referred to as "aborigines" and "natives." The image of the Protectorate peoples that persisted in the minds of many Creoles was that evoked by memories of the time when thousands of Temne, Susu, and Mende tribesmen migrated to Freetown for work, accepting lower wages and living under distinctly less privileged circumstances than the Creoles. There was a time when bands of Creole ruffians went round Freetown looking for Protectorate residents to be dragged out and beaten.[23] Since the murder in 1875 of Charles Smith, a Creole and the Police Clerk, by some men from the Protectorate, there had always been fear in the minds of the Creoles that Protectorate residents in Freetown were dangerous.[24]

The Creoles also described the Protectorate people as "unto whoms" in reference to the fact that they were the "heathens" to whom Christianity was being carried by the Creoles and missionaries. The Creoles made it quite clear during those early days that the people from the Protectorate were not welcome within the Colony, on any basis of equality. In 1879 at Wellington village in the Colony, the Creoles pulled down houses that had been built by Protectorate migrants and drove the people out of the village.[25] Contemptuous of the people from the Protectorate for their drumming and dancing and un-Christian habits, the Creoles considered them undesirable elements in their community. This attitude of the Creoles was condoned if not actively encouraged by the British who were rather anxious to preserve in the country Western cultural influences, including Christianity. To the British therefore, it was a matter of great satisfaction that the Creoles were turning out to be such capable and willing agents of Western civilization and colonialism.

In the Protectorate, the Creoles were not received with any stronger affection than they lavished on the tribesmen in the Colony. The Protectorate peoples regarded the Creoles, who were mainly traders, teachers, and missionaries, as an alien group which had renounced their African origins. Yet there was a certain ambivalence in

Protectorate attitudes towards the Creoles. On the one hand, they saw them as exploiters in trade and business and agents of European civilization in their role as teachers and missionaries. On the other hand, the Protectorate tribes somehow admired the Creoles for their progressive ways and for their ability to copy so closely the Europeans. The Protectorate tribes grouped the Creoles and Europeans as aliens and agents of foreign influence in their country.

Through the years prior to the annexation of the Sierra Leone Protectorate, the Creoles of the Colony and the peoples of the hinterland had lived in an atmosphere of mutual tolerance. It would be mistaken to describe the relationship as one of open hostility because it was not. As a matter of fact, the Creoles soon set themselves up as patrons of the underprivileged tribal peoples. It had long been a common practice among Creoles to bring up Protectorate children in their households, educating and "civilizing" them. Creole lawyers often went to great lengths to obtain justice from the British for the Protectorate peoples. Their leaders and politicians often made Protectorate causes their own and prosecuted them with the same vigor they exerted on Creole problems. Many Creoles recognized it to be their solemn duty to bring "salvation" and education to the Protectorate. But in all their endeavors, the Creoles operated on the assumption that Western value standards were inherently desirable and superior and that the Protectorate peoples should renounce their tribal practices and accept the Western standards, including Christianity, which they themselves had accepted. Maybe the real dilemma existed in this particular issue. In many areas of their personal lives, the Creoles behaved like tribal Africans. Their customs and mores had strong elements of tribal behavior patterns. Yet they professed a code of official behavior in their quest for "civilization" that produced a certain hypocrisy and ambivalence in their attitudes. The Protectorate people, on the other hand, preserved their "Africanness" and were in no way apologetic for their background and their customs.

Underneath the appearance of tolerance that characterized the relationship between the two groups was a definite mood of quiet antagonism which erupted into violence from time to time. On many occasions the Creoles were set upon by their hosts in the Protectorate and roughly treated. The climax was reached two years after the annexation in the 1898 Hut Tax War.

In many ways, the events of the Hut Tax War dramatized the

dilemma of the Creoles in their relationship with the peoples of the Protectorate. The war which began as a revolt in the Protectorate against a compulsory hut taxation turned out to be the bloodiest grand-scale massacre that had ever bathed Sierra Leone. When the British proposed the taxation, the Freetown Creoles wholeheartedly threw their weight in support of the Protectorate peoples' resistance. The press in Freetown was most vociferous in denouncing the tax and the Freetown women engaged in demonstrations outside Government House in protest. At first the Creoles in the Protectorate also refused to pay.[26] Yet, when the revolt did occur, it was directed as much against the Creoles as the Europeans. Since the attack was against all aliens, the Creoles, who had long been identified with the Europeans, qualified for alien treatment and were jointly blamed for all accumulated grievances—including the imposition of a foreign government and a foreign religion. They were remembered as agents of colonial expansion in Sierra Leone, and the occasion was used to settle long outstanding grudges.

Even Creoles who had been settled in the Protectorate for generations did not escape the avalanche. Thousands perished in the war. The hate and fears of all the years between Creoles of the Colony and the peoples of the Protectorate descended upon the Creoles in this one supreme effort to rid the country of undesirable foreign influence.[27] As a final irony, in spite of having endured the brunt of suffering, the Creoles came in for heavy blame by Cardew, the British colonial governor, who accused them of instigating the rebellion and inciting the people of the Protectorate against paying taxes.[28]

Not unnaturally, the Creoles from this time began to resent the treatment they received from the British. Further, as if to make up to the Protectorate peoples for previous acts of injustice, the British from this time seemed to embark on a deliberate policy of appeasement towards them. Steps were now taken to rectify the imbalance in educational opportunities. The British increasingly treated the Creoles as though they were responsible for all the ills in the country, and after the death of Sir Samuel Lewis, the distinguished Creole lawyer and statesman, the final vestiges of partnership in government between the British and the Creoles disappeared.[29] With the emergence of the power of the people of the Protectorate, the Creoles who had played brilliant roles in the expansion of trade, education, Christianity, and other Western European influences—not only throughout the hinterland of Sierra Leone but all along the West Coast of Africa—now painfully saw their influence on the wane.

Thus the beginning of the twentieth century found the Creoles of the Colony proud, educated, sophisticated in Western culture, but deeply resentful. They clung to a glorious past which was rapidly disappearing. They directed much of their resentment against the peoples of the Protectorate who were emerging to pose a serious challenge. From now on, the Creoles tended to oppose all new legislation and seemed to regard change as essentially detrimental to their group interests. In particular, this attitude characterized the rancor and bitterness of the Creole attacks on the 1924 Constitution. It was unfortunate that during this debate, besides expressing distrust and suspicion of British intentions, the Creoles, describing the Protectorate peoples as aliens, questioned the ability of the chiefs to operate as independent agents in the Legislative Council. In fact, even after the 1924 constitution had been imposed, the Creoles continued to derogate the performance of the chiefs, particularly in the Legislative Council.

By the time of the 1947 constitutional proposals, however, the people of the Protectorate had made sufficient educational strides to enable them to challenge the Creoles on their own level—which unfortunately meant on the same platform of prejudice and distrust. Instead of conducting a serious discussion on the constitutional proposals, the leaders of both groups plunged into vituperative exchanges which had little to do with the real issues and much to do with the suspicion and distrust each group felt for the other. Each side described the other as foreigners—the Creoles clinging to the claim of a superior legal status as British subjects, and the Protectorate peoples invoking their superior claim to the land of their forefathers.

The introduction of democracy had ensured that the Protectorate, with more than 90 percent of the population, was bound to command a majority of parliamentary seats. Awareness of this fact drove some of the Creole politicians into a state of near hysteria. They could not conceive of a situation in which the peoples of the Protectorate, whom they had always regarded as inferior, would dominate a legislature making laws that applied also to Colony Creoles. The Creoles had believed that they were more "prepared" for democracy than the peoples of the Protectorate, and they seriously believed they had special interests to protect, interests derived from their ancestral background dating from the first settlement of freed slaves in the Colony. When it became apparent that the British were determined to concede the principle of "one man one vote" to the Protectorate, the Creoles felt betrayed. They recognized this development to be the last losing round in their fight to preserve a position of superiority in the country. They still fought desperately to salvage their position, but it was much too late.

It was no longer possible to contain the antagonism of the two groups. From the date of the implementation of the 1951 constitution politics in Sierra Leone came to be overshadowed by the conflicts and confrontations of the Colony-Protectorate issue. Perhaps the most bitter of the Creoles' many complaints was inequality they claimed they suffered under the law relating to land. Whereas land in the Colony is alienable and can be held in fee simple,[30] land in the Protectorate is inalienable and cannot be so held but can only be leased, since it is vested in the chief and his tribal authorities who hold it as trustees for the people. Because of this, to the extreme chagrin of the Colony Creoles, people from the Protectorate are able to purchase land in the Colony while the Colony Creoles cannot do so in the Protectorate. In reality, the difference exists in the details of the land laws of the two areas. However, the Creoles have always considered it to be discriminatory. The question of land has always excited great emotional reactions among Creoles since they believed their ancestors had been given special rights when they first settled in Sierra Leone.

With these problems unresolved, the British proceeded to accelerate progress toward the independence of Sierra Leone. By 1961, when the country achieved independence, no positive measures had been adopted to regularize the situation and equate the laws relating to land in the two parts of the country. It is clear that these anomalies should have been removed before independence to facilitate the introduction of a uniform system of government over the whole country, but they were not.

When once it was manifest that independence was in the offing, political cleavage in the country between the Colony and the Protectorate became pronounced. All political activities were now invested with an air of urgency. It seemed important that outstanding issues should be settled before independence, after which everyone agreed changes would become more difficult.

In 1950, the Creoles had formed their own political party which they called the National Council of the Colony of Sierra Leone (N.C.C.S.L.). From the very name, with its emphasis on the Colony, the founders made it clear that the party's main aim was to champion Creole interests against what they considered to be a challenge from the Protectorate. Those Creoles who still hoped to utilize democratic processes to make their case rallied round the N.C.C.S.L. to contest the 1951 general elections—the elections which returned the first legislature with an African unofficial majority. Other Creoles, no doubt disenchanted with the democratic process, took the extreme position of boycotting the elections and challenging the legality of a constitution that provided for a legislature with an "alien" majority presuming to legislate for British subjects. The Creoles had their representatives in the new legislature table a motion in 1951, of course rejected, which called for immediate independence for the Colony.[31] The distaste of the Creoles for a proper understanding with the Protectorate peoples led some of them in the decade immediately preceding independence to pursue openly and vigorously a separatist policy rather than contemplate independence in one country which would include both elements. This attitude was not confined to debates in the legislature. It was fiercely advocated throughout the country—in the press, on political platforms, and in the courts. In fact, at the very time when independence was being celebrated in Sierra Leone, there was pending before the Privy Council in England a court action brought by the extremist Creole Settlers' Group which questioned the legality of the constitutional instruments granting independence.

The Sierra Leone People's Party (S.L.P.P.), formed in 1951 to advance the interests of Protectorate peoples, was the Protectorate riposte to the Creole National Council. It traded vituperation and invective with the National Council, and its leaders proved themselves to be past masters in the business of inflaming group passions. The general elections that followed later that year served only to harden the positions of the two groups as it gave control of the legislature, for the first time in the country's history, to a Protectorate-dominated party—the S.L.P.P.

The political confrontation of the two groups continued relentlessly through the decade that preceded independence. The National Council for the Colony of Sierra Leone, with its narrow

Creole appeal and unwillingness to contest seats in the Protectorate, ran out of steam soon after its resounding defeat at the polls. It gave way to the United Progressive Party (U.P.P.) with its wider appeal to the whole country as the main vehicle for Colony Creole protest. The Colony Creoles gave it almost overwhelming support and worked themselves into a political frenzy in the hope that it would defeat the S.L.P.P. in the 1957 general elections. By the time of these elections however, relations between the two groups had deteriorated so much that politicians of both groups openly campaigned on the Colony-Protectorate issue. The Protectorate-dominated S.L.P.P. inflicted a crushing defeat on the U.P.P. and thus formed the government that took Sierra Leone first to the status of internal self-government and later into independence

The Creoles as a group never really recovered from the humiliation of this last defeat although they made another strong effort when, after the Independence Constitutional Conference in London in 1960 and following the defection of Siaka Stevens from the independence United National Front coalition, the All People's Congress was formed. As the sole aim of this party was to supersede the S.L.P.P., once again the Colony Creoles rushed to fill its ranks in the hope of frustrating the Protectorate-dominated S.L.P.P. Once again, the hopes of the Creoles were dashed. The British granted independence without a general election and Milton Margai, the hero of the Protectorate who had led his group in confrontation with the Creoles, became the first Prime Minister of Sierra Leone.

The Independence Constitution of 1961 included a section on Fundamental Human Rights, discussed in Chapter 3, which was doubtless expected, as the British argued, to ensure the protection of the special rights the Creoles maintained would be jeopardized by implementation of the Constitution. It was soon demonstrated, however, that these provisions were hardly adequate to cope with the fundamental and deep-rooted problems generated by the Colony-Protectorate issue. The Creoles' bitter opposition to the S.L.P.P. did not abate. Many still pinned their hopes on the possibility that the A.P.C. would win the next general elections then due in 1962. As the A.P.C. also had a great following from other groups in the country, particularly from the Temnes and other tribes from the northern provinces, it seemed a reasonable expectation. But Milton Margai and the S.L.P.P. triumphed again in 1962.

Milton Margai was a man of quiet demeanor and almost apologetic public image. He cloaked his determination and political cunning in a deceptive self-effacing manner. Even though many Creoles resented him as a Mende man in supreme leadership of their beloved Sierra Leone, his personally unaggressive style conformed to the image of the submissive humble Mende man that the Creoles preferred to cling to for all Protectorate peoples. Milton Margai never really ruffled Creoles after independence, he accommodated them. When the first Governor-General, the former British Colonial Governor, retired, Margai appointed Sir Henry Lightfoot-Boston, a distinguished Creole lawyer, as Head of State. In the Judiciary, important diplomatic posts, and civil service, leading positions were assigned to Creoles. Sir Milton's policy was marked with compromise and unaggressive ineffectiveness. By the time of his death in 1964, it seemed as though the wounds of the Creoles had been healed and a detente between the Creoles and the Protectorate peoples finally reached.

This detente, if it really could have been described as such, was not destined to last. Milton Margai was succeeded by his younger brother Albert, a determined, dynamic and charismatic personality, who in many ways was everything Milton Margai was not. Albert Margai had risen to the heights of Sierra Leone politics as a champion of Protectorate causes and had been the first Protectorate man personally to challenge and confront the Creoles. Soon after he returned home from his legal studies in Britain, he raised Creole eyebrows by daring to contest the Legislative Council elections of 1948 for a Freetown seat which the Creoles had always regarded as their sacred preserve. To the Creoles, this was a most presumptuous affront from a Mende man from the Protectorate and they closed their ranks to defeat him. Albert Margai then plunged with tremendous energy into the political organization of the Protectorate peoples both in the Colony and in the Protectorate. The establishment and subsequent strength of the S.L.P.P. owed much to his political skill. In fact, it is accurate to state that the emergence of Albert Margai as a political leader coincided with the emergence of the Protectorate peoples as a dominant political force in Sierra Leone. The Creoles soon came to identify Albert Margai with the Protectorate and reserved for him a particular hatred as the evil genius behind what they considered the Protectorate threat.

Nevertheless, the Creoles seemed at first to rally around Albert Margai when he took over the reins of government; but they soon relapsed into their traditional opposition to Protectorate leadership. They deeply resented his personally assertive style. They feared that the dreaded Protectorate takeover was now highly probable under Albert Margai. Even though some of his closest advisers and friends were young Creole intellectuals, they saw in his determination to produce dynamic policies the assertion of Protectorate dominance.

The Creoles, after less than two years of Albert Margai's leadership, embarked on a campaign of hate and vilification which surpassed anything that had occurred before, even in the particularly scurrilous record of Colony-Protectorate feuding. Known criminals instigated by a disbarred and dishonest lawyer joined in making extreme and sometimes imaginary accusations against him. The Creole-dominated Judiciary and the Civil Service were accused of open hostility to Albert Margai. He lost confidence in these institutions and the future of good government was seriously threatened. Politically, Albert Margai's government was accused of waste, corruption, and much else. The Creoles rallied around the A.P.C. and used it as the vehicle for vigorous dissent. They also as a group led the attack on Albert Margai's administration. Many Creoles in the Judiciary and the higher grades of the Civil Service were seriously accused of using their positions for subversive activities against Albert Margai's government and of both open and secret support of the opposition. The Creoles were really spoiling for a fight and a showdown. They still hoped to destroy the Protectorate ascendancy which Albert Margai represented in their eyes and could hardly wait for the next general elections to pour out their frustrations and resentment through the ballot box. In this, the Creoles were helped by the decline of the S.L.P.P. as a powerful political force. Badly organized, it had gradually appeared to be a tribal party for the Mendes. Confronted with the better organized A.P.C. under Siaka Stevens, the S.L.P.P. was left with predominantly Mende support while almost all the other tribes threw their lot with the A.P.C.

True to form, when the 1967 general elections finally came, the Creoles went to the polls in their thousands in an unprecedented display of political fervor, and inflicted a defeat in the Colony area on Albert Margai's party's candidates. The Creole-supported A.P.C. won every contested seat in the Colony area and dramatized in an unforgettable fashion their desperate anxiety to be rid of Albert Margai and what they thought he represented. The story of course was quite different in the provinces where Albert Margai's S.L.P.P. won almost every seat in the Mende area.

The 1967 elections produced a deadlock. Sir Henry Lightfoot-Boston, the distinguished Creole Governor-General, constantly exposed to Creole pressures and influence, resolved the deadlock in favor of the A.P.C. and appointed its leader, Siaka Stevens, Prime Minister. A *coup d'état* followed. There are many who believed that the whole tragic series of events leading to the *coup d'état* would never have taken place but for the Colony-Protectorate problem.

Many Creoles at first openly welcomed the military takeover and applauded it as the regime that ousted Albert Margai and his S.L.P.P. They publicly gloated at the antics of half-illiterate army and police officers who constituted the National Reformation Council.[32] Like the intoxicated French peasants who crowded the *ad hoc* tribunals that sent men to the guillotine during the French Revolution, many Creoles, particularly women, reserved their daily front seats, cheering and jeering as occasion demanded, when the illegal Kangaroo Courts which assumed the dubious respectability of Commissions of Inquiry conducted their mocking sessions. Once again, the Creoles were having a field day, or so they thought. The public pillorying and slaughter of leaders of the Proctectorate-dominated S.L.P.P. was sweet indeed to the Creole taste. There were those who saw in the fact that the chairmen of the various Commissions were Creoles, and in the subsequent anti-Mende flavor of Albert Margai's public humiliation, additional evidence of strong anti-Protectorate feelings instigated by the Creoles.

However, when in April 1968, a year after the military takeover, civilian rule was restored under the A.P.C. with Siaka Stevens as Prime Minister, the Creoles were jubilant indeed. They no doubt saw in the new government their greatest opportunity to restore Creole influence to its former place of prominence in Sierra Leone politics. They have given their full support to the A.P.C. government's extremely vindictive persecution of former S.L.P.P. leaders and prominent supporters. It has, of course, been useful for the time being for all groups to close ranks against the dominant Mendes and their friends. How long the Creoles will continue in harmonious relationship with their newly acquired political allies is another matter. I suspect that this alliance will not long endure. If the history of the Colony-Protectorate relationship is any guide, it will not take the Creoles long to find themselves relapsing into their traditional bitter opposition of all non-Creole leadership. What exact character the next phase of the Colony-Protectorate struggle will assume is yet to be seen. Already, however, it is possible to discern a growing closeness and recognition of identity of interests among all Protectorate tribes. It seems as though the Temnes and the other dissident tribes are now drawing closer to the Mendes to reveal the Creoles as the real villains of the piece. If this development continues, the Creoles will be facing again a situation similar to that of 1957. This would be sad for the Creoles who should know that in any confrontation with the Protectorate peoples on one side and themselves on the other, the Creoles can never win. The implementation of democracy in Sierra Leone has ensured this. Perhaps their dwindling numbers and the march of time will eliminate the Creoles as a political force worth serious reckoning. This again will be a pity, because the Creoles have contributed so much to the culture and the dynamics of progress in Sierra Leone and should have been able to continue to do so if the Colony-Protectorate issue had not been allowed to deteriorate into the vexing problem it has become in the history of the country.

## NOTES

1. Christopher Fyfe, *History of Sierra Leone,* p. 541.
2. James Somerset Case, 1772. In this case, Lord Mansfield declared slavery to be contrary to the laws of England.
3. Granville Town was named in honor of Granville Sharp, the leading founder of the settlement. Fyfe, *op. cit.,* p. 20.
4. Arthur T. Porter, *op. cit.,* p. 11.
5. Christopher Fyfe, *op. cit.,* p. 79.
6. Porter, *op. cit.,* p. 11.
7. Christopher Fyfe, *op. cit.,* p. 19.
8. The Temne Chief King Tom sold two settlers who annoyed him to a passing French ship. Hoare, *Memoirs of Granville Sharp.*
9. Christopher Fyfe, *op. cit.,* p. 69. "Children sent by chiefs paid nothing and were lodged."
10. *Ibid.,* p. 26.
11. *Ibid.,* p. 100.

12. In 1825 Turner, the Governor, deposed a chief whose policy he considered to be against the interests of Macaulay, a British trader, and installed another more satisfactory to him. *Ibid.*, p. 157.

13. *Ibid.*, p. 255.

14. *Ibid.*, p. 299.

15. *Ibid.*, p. 374.

16. *Ibid.*, p. 277. In 1855, the British sent a primitive military expedition to Maligia near Binti and were soundly routed leaving seventy-seven killed, drowned, or taken prisoner.

17. *Ibid.*, p. 482.

18. *Ibid.* When the police caught men looting a town in the interior, they seized and flogged them, arrested their leader, tied him with ropes, and sent him to jail in Freetown where he soon died from the ulcerated bruises sustained from the ropes.

19. *Sierra Leone Gazette,* August 31, 1896.

20. Christopher Fyfe, *op. cit.,* p. 541.

21. *Ibid.*, p. 109.

22. K. L. Little, *The Mende of Sierra Leone,* p. 53.

23. Christopher Fyfe, *op. cit.,* p. 455.

24. *Ibid.*

25. *Ibid.*

26. *Ibid.*, p. 560.

27. *Ibid.*, p. 572.

28. *Ibid.*, p. 579.

29. *Ibid.*, p. 617.

30. "Fee simple"—land held—full legal possession to which owner enjoys complete title.

31. Sierra Leone Legislative Council Debates, Session 1951–1952 (Freetown, 1953).

32. The National Reformation Council was the name adopted by the military and police senior officers who staged a *coup d'état* and assumed full power in Sierra Leone on March 23, 1967.

# CHAPTER 6

# Tribalism in Sierra Leone

In contemporary African politics, "tribalism" has become an emotive word with certain distinctive connotations. Its general use is in connection with problems that have developed among various tribes and tribal groups in African countries in their relations with each other. These problems assumed political and contemporary significance during the period of colonialism. Even though colonialism as such could not be said to have created all of them, yet by the very nature of colonialism itself, some aspects of the problems were fostered and others created. In any event, colonialism did little to eradicate them and they have remained to plague independent African countries long after the yoke of colonialism has been removed.[1]

The system of government that colonialism inevitably imposed on an unwilling collection of tribes was bound to generate tensions among such tribes in their dealings with each other. These tribes in many cases had been aware of each other's existence only as foes. Living in small restricted communities, due largely to the impenetrability of the tropical forests, the only type of contact with other tribes that individual tribes had been able to understand had been that derived from warfare. The social and community unit that mattered was that of the tribe. Anyone not belonging to the tribe was regarded as a stranger. Any notion of intertribal relationship under a common overlord was remote and almost inconceivable.

What these tribes were able to understand from tradition and experience was a relationship with an overlord to whom fealty was payable and to whom military service might be given if this was considered necessary. Whatever relationship the overlord might enjoy with any vassal tribe did not affect his relationship with other tribes with whom he might enjoy a similar relationship. Besides, so long as a vassal tribe fulfilled its obligations to the overlord, such a tribe was left well alone to conduct its own domestic affairs. There was no question of any interest on the part of the overlord in preserving any sort of law or order within a vassal tribe, or in teaching such tribes "democracy" or any "isms" relating to forms of government.

But colonialism changed the picture. Sitting in conference rooms in faraway Europe, colonial powers arbitrarily, without much reference to ethnic, linguistic, or tribal realities, partitioned Africa, and thus created new countries comprising many tribes that had very little in common and in some cases, had had previously hostile relationships. This partitioning of Africa often left members of the same tribe in different countries after partition.

The experience of Sierra Leone is in many ways similar to that of many other West African countries. When the boundaries of Sierra Leone were determined, little or no attention was paid to tribal distribution in the country. The dominating considerations were the interests of the French and the British. After years of disputes between the two European nations over their respective spheres of influence in this part of Africa, their representatives met in Paris in January 1895 and quite arbitrarily fixed the boundary line between Sierra Leone and French Guinea. The delimitation followed almost entirely geographical lines. Such scanty regard was paid to tribal realities, for example, that the boundary divided the people of Samu chiefdom, an important Temne chiefdom in the Northern Province —half in French Guinea, and the other half in Sierra Leone. On the Liberian border, the boundary settlement imposed by the British on the weak young Liberian Republic in 1882, after years of wrangling, left some of the Gallinas Mende tribe in Liberia and others in Sierra Leone.[2]

Within the territory of Sierra Leone itself, there are at least fifteen tribal or ethnic groups. The Mendes who live mainly in the South, numbering over 800,000 and the Temnes who live mainly in the North, with over 600,000 are the two largest tribal groups. The other major tribal groups number around 200,000 each.[3] The Creoles total less than 40,000.

Before the independence of Sierra Leone, the image of the tribe was symbolized by the person of the chief who governed the tribe with the help of elders later known as Tribal Authorities. The identity of the tribe was preserved through the use of its own language and the veneration of its particular tribal customs and traditions. These customs and traditions related mainly to domestic and family aspects of daily life. The responsibility for the defense of the tribe against foreign invasions was left to the chief who had full authority to mobilize his people for tribal warfare. Since warfare was the supreme involvement that could engage the tribe, the personality of the group was always best expressed through its participation in war. The enemy, of course, was always some other tribe. The bellicose and tribal instincts which such involvements generated can usefully be compared with the modern idea of patriotism as understood in the national situation. In the tribal context, loyalty to the group and the willingness of the individual to pay the supreme sacrifice for its survival can properly be described as "tribalism."

But there is another sense in which the word "tribalism" has been used increasingly in recent times. This meaning is related to the more fierce and partisan emotional manifestation of tribal interests in the political context. With the end of the era of tribal wars, came the period of modern political activities. As in many other African countries, colonization in Sierra Leone ushered in, however slowly, democratic institutions. It also brought in a system of centralized government which gradually assumed a unitary character. With the progress of decolonization in Sierra Leone and the advance toward independence, these democratic processes soon gathered enough momentum to rock the very foundations of traditional tribal life symbolized in the person of the chief. Under colonialism, the chief preserved much of his traditional authority and in some ways he was even able to strengthen the basis of his power. Even though the colonial authority and presence in the country was maintained through the colonial Governor and his District Commissioners, tribal cohesion was essentially preserved since the individuals within the tribe recognized no other real authority outside the tribe. But with the introduction of democratic institutions and the establishment of a centralized and unitary form of government, the need to galvanize tribal political activities around new objectives became imperative. Hitherto, tribal political activities other than acts directed externally against rival tribes and warring opponents were confined to family and factional rivalries over chieftaincy succession. With the implementation of a centralized and unitary system of government, as well as with the introduction of parliamentary democracy, also came the establishment of national political parties. It then became immediately apparent to tribal groups that the new vehicle through which they could best pursue their tribal interests was the national political party.

The history of political parties in Sierra Leone clearly demonstrates the extent to which tribal groups utilized political parties before and after independence as vehicles for the pursuit of tribal interests. In this context of political group identity, the Creoles could well be regarded as a tribal group, since they exhibited all the identifiable group instincts recognizable in the indigenous tribes of Sierra Leone whenever they felt their interests threatened by other groups in the country.

When once the 1947 constitutional proposals had been introduced and it became apparent that independence was imminent, party politics emerged in full stature and immediately became identified with tribal group interests. As long as the struggle for independence remained vague and spontaneous, all the political elements in the country joined forces in the independence movement to rid themselves of their British colonial masters. But as soon as independence became a real possibility, tribal group interests predominated, and the animosities were no longer directed against the British only, but against any tribal group within the country likely to emerge as the dominant group after independence. This behavior is in fact a characteristic feature of tribal politics in Africa. Several tribal groups are often willing to join forces against a group they consider to be a common opponent. As soon as the common foe has been vanquished, this temporary unity tends to break down and the former constituent tribes pursue once more only those objectives considered vital to their own narrow interests.

Thus in Sierra Leone, when the tribal groups joined issue over the 1947 constitutional proposals, the political elements that had formerly coalesced to demand independence for the country disintegrated again into tribal interest groups. The first combination had all the Protectorate tribes on one side, and the Creole tribal group on the other. One therefore finds the National Council for the Colony of Sierra Leone being formed in 1950 to advocate and defend Creole tribal interests—interests seen by the Protectorate tribes to constitute a threat to their position. Accordingly, the Protectorate tribes closed ranks and formed the Sierra Leone People's Party as the political organization and vehicle for the prosecution of the group interests of all the Protectorate tribes. In the 1951 general elections for the implementation of the first widely representative constitution, the major political issue had tribal overtones which found open expression in the Colony-Protectorate issue. In this instance, the Creole tribal group interests were pitched against the common group interests of all the Protectorate tribes. The results of the elections clearly showed that tribalism in these terms was a powerful factor in the politics of the country. The National Council for the Colony of Sierra Leone won all but one [4] of the Colony seats and the Sierra Leone People's Party swept all the Protectorate seats as well as winning one in the Colony. These results only hardened the positions of both groups and from then on tribalism developed into the most formidable single factor in Sierra Leone politics.

This particular pattern of the tribalist fight in Sierra Leone reached a climax in the 1957 general elections which, turning out to be the last before independence, developed into a full-scale confrontation between the Protectorate tribes supporting the S.L.P.P. and the Creoles supporting the newly formed United Progressive Party. After its defeat in 1951, the National Council for the Colony of Sierra Leone had been replaced by the more dynamic United Progressive Party as the leading political organization championing Creole interests. Although the U.P.P. enjoyed a wider following because it was able to attract some support from the northern tribes, the S.L.P.P. remained unchallenged as the dominant custodian of Protectorate interests and hopes. The S.L.P.P overwhelmed the U.P.P. at the polls and established once and for all that the Creoles, operating politically as a tribal group, can be no match against the Protectorate tribes in any political confrontation. And so, in the last general elections before independence, political parties were used largely as vehicles for the rallying of tribal allegiances and pursuit of tribal interests. The general elections of 1951 and 1957 were noticeably lacking in any other issues.

The antagonisms of tribalism in Sierra Leone politics have not been restricted to those between the Creoles and the Protectorate tribes. In the history of the country, the Mendes of the South as the largest tribal group and the Temnes of the North as the second largest tribal group have always been great rivals. This rivalry had often erupted into hostility and violence in the period before coloni-

zation and the annexation of the Protectorate. During this early period, there were also rivalries among other minor tribes like the Susus
and the Fulas. From time to time various tribal combinations emerged
to confront a particular tribal group that was considered too powerful
and was regarded as posing a threat to the interests of the others.
After the introduction of democratic institutions and a centralized
system of government, this tendency for the establishment of *ad hoc*
coalitions continued only now within the framework of political
parties.

Although the Sierra Leone People's Party had won its spurs as
the champion of Protectorate tribal interests and its early executive
committee leadership had included prominent Temne leaders, the
Temnes had always been uncomfortable within the ranks of the
S.L.P.P. The reason for this was that the Mendes dominated not only
the leadership of the party but also its grass roots. The Margai
brothers, Milton and Albert, were scions of a prominent Mende
family and a number of the other more prominent leaders of the
S.L.P.P. had been drawn from that tribe. True, some Temne leaders
had been given prominent positions in the S.L.P.P., but the Margais—
first Milton, then Albert—had made sure through their personal
political leadership that the supreme berth was reserved for the Mendes. This situation caused a growing impatience among the Temnes,
their tribal affinities making them susceptible to the attractions of any
political party which was not so dominated by their arch rivals. Thus,
when the United Progressive Party was established in 1955, it was
able to attract an impressive following from the northern Temnes.
Many Temnes, no doubt, saw in the U.P.P. an organ through which
to express their resentment and protest concerning the Mende ascendancy through the S.L.P.P. However, sufficient numbers of the old-
guard Temne politicians remained with the S.L.P.P. to bring about
its defeat of the U.P.P. in 1957. The Creole tribal group was still regarded by the majority of Protectorate tribes, including the Temnes,
as the most formidable opponent threatening their group tribal interests.

After the rout of the U.P.P. at the polls in 1957, the point of
Protectorate tribal ascendancy had been made, and the Temnes be-
came still more restless and dissatisfied with the situation in the
S.L.P.P. An opportunity for the use of another political party for the

expression of non-Mende tribal interests came with the establishment of the All People's Congress in 1960.

The People's National Party (P.N.P.) had been formed in 1958, as described in Chapter 3, by Albert Margai who led a group of dissidents out of the S.L.P.P. and was joined by intellectuals and young Turks from many other tribal groups, even including Creoles. For a while, it appeared very likely that the P.N.P. would become the leading party in the country. However, before the P.N.P. could test its strength in a general election, it was dissolved following the creation of the United National Front coalition of all the political parties in Sierra Leone immediately before independence. As has already been stated, Siaka Stevens, a man of one of the northern tribes [5] and the deputy leader of the P.N.P., declined to join the coalition of the United National Front, and took with him into still another new party, the All People's Congress (A.P.C.), most of the non-Mende elements of the erstwhile P.N.P. It is significant that when the P.N.P. disintegrated, the bulk of its Mende following, led by Albert Margai, happily returned to the ranks of the Mende-dominated S.L.P.P., while the non-Mende members rallied around Siaka Stevens in his new A.P.C. It is also significant that the Creoles flocked to the A.P.C. All non-Mende tribal groups now seemed to recognize in the A.P.C. a convenient political vehicle through which their tribal group interests could best be served.

At this juncture in Sierra Leone politics, a realignment of tribal groupings was clearly taking place. Since the Mendes, because of their dominance of the governing S.L.P.P., were seen to be the group to beat, all the other tribal groups saw their advantage in uniting against them. Thus in the nineteen-sixties the political party organizations in confrontation in Sierra Leone were the S.L.P.P. and the A.P.C. This also amounted to a confrontation of the Mendes and the other tribal groups. This analysis, of course, reflects the situation in broad and general terms. There were those in Sierra Leone who gave support to political parties for personal and other reasons without conforming to any tribal group tendency. But such were few and not enough to affect to any noticeable extent the general pattern.

In the general elections of 1962—the first after independence—the S.L.P.P. and the A.P.C. were the contestant parties. Even though the S.L.P.P. was able to keep a few seats in the Creole and Temne areas, it was the overwhelming support it received from the Mende area that kept it in power. The new coalition of the Creoles and the Temnes and other northern tribal groups nearly succeeded in wresting power from the Mende-dominated S.L.P.P. in this election.

The process of alienation of all non-Mende tribal elements from the governing S.L.P.P. was completed in the years between the general elections of 1962 and 1967. The atmosphere in which the 1967 elections campaign was conducted was charged with tribal group animosities, particularly in the Colony area. The results demonstrated most eloquently the extent of tribal cleavage in the country. In the Colony area and in the northern provinces, the Creoles, Temnes, Limbas, and other minority tribal groups voted overwhelmingly for the A.P.C., which won nearly all the seats in these areas. The Mendes kept faith with the S.L.P.P. and gave it the usual loyal support, returning almost all the seats in their area for the S.L.P.P. Thus the general elections resulted in a dead heat or a near dead heat; the combinations of tribal allegiances were such as to produce a stalemate when the results of the 1967 general elections finally came through.

It is particularly interesting to observe that in the Government Statement on the Dove-Edwin Commission of Inquiry into the Conduct of the 1967 General Elections,[6] the following comments were made on the results of the elections:

> The 1967 results showed sectional alignment throughout the country. The Sierra Leone People's Party was confined to the Southern Province, Kailahun and Kenema Districts and part of the Kono District in the Eastern Province; the All People's Congress was confined largely to the Northern Province and the then Western area.[7]

The areas referred to as S.L.P.P. strongholds, namely the Southern Province and the Kailahun and Kenema Districts, are all in the Mende tribal area. The Kono district, with a large intertribal population, voted half S.L.P.P. and half A.P.C. The areas of A.P.C. strength, namely the Northern Province and the Western area, are peopled by non-Mende tribes.

In another paragraph of the same report, the Government Statement continued:

There was a sudden upsurge of tribal feelings when the announcement of the final results was delayed. This would have developed into a tribal war if the National Reformation Council had not stepped in on the 23rd March, 1967.[8]

It is quite clear from these statements that in the view of the National Reformation Council, which was then the government, the 1967 general elections had exposed once again the dangerous state of tribal tensions and feelings in Sierra Leone.

The Governor-General, Sir Henry Lightfoot-Boston, was evidently aware of the gravity of the crisis that immediately developed as a direct result of this tribal voting. He bluntly expressed his fears on this score to Albert Margai and Siaka Stevens, the leaders of the two parties, on March 20, 1967, when he suggested that a coalition government be formed to avert a tribal confrontation. Unfortunately, this advice was rejected, and the country was later plunged into a crisis of the first magnitude.

When on March 21, 1967, the Governor-General yielded to pressures from the Colony Creole elements and appointed Siaka Stevens, Prime Minister, events dramatically reached a climax. Brigadier David Lansanna, the Force Commander, detained the Governor-General and the new Prime Minister under house arrest and declared martial law. Democracy and constitutionality were in ruins in Sierra Leone and the first experiment at nation building had collapsed.

There are those who trace this rapid deterioration and breakdown of constitutionality in Sierra Leone to tribalism. In support of this contention, they cite the fact that the Governor-General and those who pressured him were all Creoles and that his decision was in favor of the Creole-supported A.P.C., after he himself had recognized the tribalist overtones of the elections. They also cite the fact that Brigadier Lansanna, himself a Mende, used the Mende-dominated army to intervene and halt the pendulum which then appeared to be swinging in favor of the Creoles and the other minority tribes.

Thus tribalism contributed in no little measure to the breakdown of the democratic process in Sierra Leone. What the Governor-General realized on the eve of the breakdown ought to have been already apparent to any astute student of politics in West Africa: that the political parties and the entire machinery of democratic institutions were being used as convenient vehicles for the expression and promotion of tribalism.

This development raises serious questions as to the suitability of implementing Western-style democracy with the multiparty apparatus in a postcolonial African situation where there are many tribes with special tribal interests—tribes that have not had a long record of peaceful relations and coexistence through the years before the colonialist era. The problems of tribalism seem to be aggravated by the adoption of a multiparty system in a unitary state. This system has often served to perpetuate tribal cleavages, making it impossible for any one group to accept a government that is dominated by members of another tribe. In the customary atmosphere of intertribal rivalries and distrust, it has been hardly surprising to find this unwillingness of any one tribe to submit to a government with which its members do not identify. To a tribe thus left out of the government the situation smacks of colonialism. Tribal people can well understand the exercise of power by one of their own tribe as chief or ruler, but not the exercise of ministerial authority by individuals from other tribes. Colonialism, however, has come and gone and independence has arrived. Many disparate groups have found themselves living together within the same body politic with the avowed intention of building a nation. In Sierra Leone as in many other former British colonial territories, the situation in my view has been made more difficult by the adoption at independence of the multiparty system of parliamentary democracy.

Any solutions for the future for good and orderly government in Sierra Leone after such a breakdown must take full cognizance of the problems of tribalism which have bedeviled good government since independence. It is possible that the divergencies in ethnic and cultural heritage of the various tribes in Sierra Leone could well prove to be a source of richness in the nation's culture and experiences provided the proper constitutional framework exists for such intertribal cooperation.

## NOTES

1. R. W. Apple (Jr.): *The New York Times.* November 23, 1969, p. 1.
2. Christopher Fyfe, *History of Sierra Leone,* p. 431.

3. *Sierra Leone Government Provinces Hand-book,* 1961.

4. The one seat in the Colony not carried by the N.C.C.S.L. (Freetown East) was won by M. S. Mustapha, then considered a political maverick who is in fact a Muslim Creole born and raised in Freetown.

5. Siaka Stevens is generally considered to belong to the Limba tribe, one of the minor tribes of the North.

6. The military junta that assumed power in Sierra Leone in March 1967 after the breakdown of constitutional government set up the Dove-Edwin Commission of Inquiry to report on the conduct of the 1967 general elections which immediately preceded the *coup d'état.*

7. Statement of the National Reformation Council on the *Report of the Dove-Edwin Commission of Inquiry,* par. 22, *Report of the Dove-Edwin Commission,* p. 2 (Sierra Leone Government, 1967).

8. *Ibid.,* par. 23, p. 3.

# CHAPTER 7

# The Role of Chiefs in Sierra Leone

Ever since the days of the earliest European contacts with Sierra Leone, chiefs, or kings, as they were called in early records, have always played a dominant role in the affairs of the country and of their people. In the early sixteenth century when ships were attracted to the Sierra Leone estuary for watering purposes, it was with the chief of the people that the ship's captains had to deal.[1] The Manes, the name given by the early Portuguese adventurers to the then dominant tribe,[2] had their king and subkings. These natural rulers preserved law and order and enforced their complete authority over the areas they ruled. The Poro, a very ancient secret society, seems to have provided the source and the authority for royal power.[3] From the early days, women as well as men ruled over tribes; as a matter of fact, some of the most celebrated chiefs in the history of Sierra Leone have been women.

In its origins, chieftaincy seems to have developed out of the necessity for a group of people living in a settlement separate and distinct from any other to have a leader. In the circumstances of those early days, such a leader had to be a warrior. He was expected to protect his people from external forces as well as to preserve law and order within their ranks. The chief presided over a political as well as a social unit. In some cases, particularly in Temne areas, the chief was assumed to be invested with supernatural and spiritual powers and his people believed him to derive his authority from God. Even among the Mendes, where the chief was more of a secular authority, he was able through the support of the Poro secret society to enforce his will largely because of the belief of his people that he controlled forces not limited to the earthly and to the physical.

The power and authority of chiefs have always varied depending on the personality of the individual and the area of his rule. Some chiefs controlled extensive areas with many subchiefs and vassals accepting their suzerainty. Others have had control of only very small areas. In modern Sierra Leone those ruling over large areas are known as Paramount Chiefs and others are known as Chiefs, Sub-chiefs, and Section Chiefs, depending on the extent of their kingdom. However limited or extensive their authority, chiefs have always been accepted by their people as the supreme source of temporal power and authority. All political and social activities in the community flow from the chief and are directed by him. Naturally, from the earliest days, the chief was the accredited spokesman of his people. He made all the decisions for them in their external transactions and also presided over their domestic disputes, producing solutions for all their internal problems. The early European traders soon came to understand the power and authority of the chief and quickly realized that in all transactions with the people, they had to act through the chief without whose consent no arrangement was effective.

When in 1787 the first settlers sailed into the Sierra Leone harbor, and Captain Thompson sought to acquire a settlement for his band of freed slaves, it was with the Temne subchief, King Tom, that he had to negotiate, and it was from King Naimbana, the overlord Temne chief, that final approval for the cession of Sierra Leone land had to be obtained. When eventually a treaty was succesfully negotiated, the persons who represented the people and appended their marks, were all chiefs.[4]

Much of the power and authority of chiefs in tribal African societies had all the ingredients of monarchical absolutism. These chiefs, like absolute monarchs, believed their power to be derived from God, and by implication, that they were answerable only to God. They thus believed that God's intentions for the people were discernible through the will of the chiefly authoritarian ruler. In their capacity as absolute monarchs, chiefs were accorded a special authority as custodians if not owners of the land of their people.

Originally, the chief was regarded not merely as the custodian of the people's land, but as the actual owner. This concept is easily understood in the light of the historical beginnings of chieftaincy. The chief originally owed his position to personal military prowess and he maintained it largely through force of arms. His main source of economic strength was derived from the spoils of battle—slaves and plunder. On capture of a town, a chief automatically took possession of the land of the captured and carried the people off as slaves. The land became the acquisition of the victorious chief, who might leave some of his warriors behind as his vassals and representatives to hold the land on his behalf. Later, when the days of regular tribal warfare as a way of life were over and the British had come into the country, agriculture replaced warfare as the main base of the economy. From that time on, the people became more interested in holding land and no longer acquiesced in the chiefs' arbitrary exercise of sole ownership rights over all land. With the growth of uninterrupted tenure, individual ownership claims increased and the chiefs became restricted to rights of jurisdiction and arbitration—rights which were later shared with tribal authorities.[5] The chiefs thus became custodians rather than owners of the people's land.

Nowadays, in their personal capacities, the chief and his kinsmen do not technically enjoy any rights over land superior to those enjoyed by any other member of the chiefdom. To acquire land additional to what he already possesses, the chief has to submit his claim to the same processes as any other tribesman.[6] Nevertheless, the chiefs' influence as custodians over land is extremely great and it ensures for the chief a certain control and authority over the lives of his people.

The British never forgot the lessons of their early encounters with the tribes of Sierra Leone. These experiences taught them unmistakably that for the successful pursuit of their aims in the country a strong working alliance with chiefs should be established. From the inception of the Sierra Leone Protectorate, the British therefore embarked on a policy of strengthening the authority of the chiefs. Largely due, no doubt, to the authoritarian nature of chieftaincy, the people often rebelled against their leaders and situations of uncertainty and instability generally followed such occurrences. The British were of course anxious that law and order be maintained in the country to ensure the easy pursuit of their own interests. They saw in the institution of chieftaincy an established system of government through which they could operate for the implementation of their own policies. They therefore resolutely pursued a policy of collaboration and virtual alliance with the chiefs.

In furtherance of this alliance, after the establishment of the Protectorate in 1896, chiefs were allowed to preserve customary rights to tribute and labor for a considerable number of years. Laws were enacted during the British colonial era which entrenched customary rights to tribute from subchiefs and headmen, and also preserved for chiefs the enjoyment of forced labor from their subjects.[7] Even when legislation was later introduced to modify the chiefs' rights to forced labor from adult male subjects, instead of terminating it altogether such legislation simply limited it to thirty days per year and six days per week.[8] It required a full-scale riot and peasant revolt much later on to persuade the Sierra Leone government of the necessity for the final abolition of forced labor.[9] After the annexation of the Protectorate, both before and after the abolition of their rights to receive tribute, chiefs in Sierra Leone were paid salaries. At first these money payments were related to tax collection but later to the size of their chiefdoms. Politically, with the annexation of the Protectorate, chiefs were able to consolidate their position as head of the local administration. The District Commissioner, as the local representative of the British colonial central government, became the "good friend" of the chief and used the considerable power and resources of the British administrative machinery to sustain the chief's position with his people while consolidating British control of the area.

When once the British decided that they needed the preservation of indigenous tribal institutions for the successful operation of their colonial policies in the Protectorate, they embraced the office of the chieftaincy as a useful vehicle for policy implementation. They were content to preserve the chief as head of tribal life with respect to domestic and customary matters, while they kept over-all authority for maintenance of law and security and, more important still, for preservation of the kind of atmosphere within the chiefs' community that would be congenial to the furtherance of their colonial and trade interests. In this way, the British allied with the chiefs to their mutual advantage to impose authority over the people. This role played by the chiefs within the structure of colonial administration in the Protectorate enabled them to retain traditional authority and at the same time enrich themselves as privileged participants in the modern colonial economy. What turned out to be of the greatest significance, however, was that this alliance provided the chiefs with a vested interest in the perpetuation of the colonial administrative system which had brought them so many advantages. Quite apart from the financial and material benefits the colonial system in the Protectorate brought them, it also reinforced their authority over their people and, in many instances, the system sustained their oppression of the people.

The tacit alliance of the British and the chiefs came to maturity with the adoption in Sierra Leone of the policy of indirect rule known as "Native Administration." Under this system, the chiefs continued to strengthen their financial and political positions. The effect has been to further entrench the chiefs as the elite of their societies in every aspect of life.

Economically, during the period of tribute payments, the chiefs made capital of the tribute paid them in goods and services to enhance their standing in the community. This enabled them to expand their agricultural output and ensure satisfactory markets for their products. Furthermore, chiefs derived direct benefits through their control of the land-tenure system, particularly from rents and royalties paid to them on behalf of their people by foreign mining companies. Later, when tribute payments were made illegal, the salaries paid to chiefs in lieu of tribute preserved their status as the most affluent in their societies. The superior economic strength they enjoyed entrenched the chiefs not only as the most powerful economic class, but also as the socially and politically elite. With economic control virtually in their hands, they manipulated the lives of their subjects by playing the role of patrons to all—all, that is, who were willing to toe the line and submit with proper subservience to the chiefs' will. The chiefs' special proprietorship over land ensured more than any other single factor his unquestionable control over the lives and destinies of his people.

As if this were not enough, the British reserved for chiefs, in the various constitutions they gave Sierra Leone after annexation of the Protectorate, an increasingly powerful role that is unique in the history of British Commonwealth constitutions namely, a special role as spokesmen and representatives of the Protectorate in the area of central government. When in 1924 the first constitution after the establishment of the Protectorate was introduced, provisions were made for a unicameral legislature with the Colony and Protectorate represented in the same chamber. While the five representatives from the Colony were elected (three) and nominated (two) from professional and other groups without any restrictions, the constitution specifically stipulated that all three Protectorate members to be nominated should be chiefs. Thus began in Sierra Leone a process, which continued into independence and afterwards, of making chiefs the accredited spokesmen of their people in legislative as well as in other matters, even within the context of modern parliamentary democracy. From the standpoint of British colonial policy making, this approach was no doubt logical and consistent because it consolidated the chief's role not only within his community, but also as the middleman between the British and the people of the Protectorate.

After 1943, when the British decided to appoint Africans to the Executive Council for the first time, one from the Colony and one from the Protectorate, the representative from the Protectorate was always a chief. Here, again, there is evidence that in every stage in the evolution toward self-government in Sierra Leone, chiefs were made to play a decisive role in the affairs of the country. The importance of the role of chiefs in the political development of Sierra Leone was again underlined when the Protectorate Assembly was established in 1946. This Assembly was set up as a forum for the discussion of essentially Protectorate affairs and to acquaint the people of the Protectorate as a whole with the processes of parliamentary and representational government. Of a total membership of forty-two, twenty-six seats were reserved for Paramount Chiefs. In this attempt at democratizing institutions in the Protectorate, the British took pains to ensure that the chiefs' influence and power emerged predominant in the new Assembly. Of the remaining sixteen seats, eleven were reserved for government department officials, one each for European and Creole business interest groups, one for missionary interests, and only two for educated nonchief Protectorate Africans who were to be selected by Native Administrations, organizations over which chiefs exercised considerable influence.

Inevitably, the growing educated group of Protectorate youth resented this dominance of chiefs, particularly in political matters. The developing group conflict between the chiefs and the peasants now and again erupted into violence and riots which became subjects of hastily set up Commissions of Inquiry. Yet the natural loyalty of the people of the Protectorate toward the office of the chieftaincy in the final analysis preserved the institution even though individual chiefs were often deposed. This ambivalence stems from a time-honored respect all Protectorate persons feel for the chief as a symbol of group unity and of tribal pride combined with an acute awareness of the oppressiveness of his rule and the system generally.

Even after considerable pressure was applied by the educated elements in the Protectorate for greater democratization of the Protectorate Assembly, the major political Protectorate institution, the number of nonchief members in this organization was raised only from two to six.

The same pattern emerged when the all important 1947 constitutional proposals, which for the first time provided for an unofficial African majority in the legislature, still preserved for the chiefs the controlling voice, not only for the determination of Protectorate representation but also for African representation as a whole. Under these proposals, the Protectorate was given thirteen seats against seven for the Colony. Twelve of the thirteen seats allocated were to be filled by elections from the chief-dominated Protectorate Assembly and the thirteenth seat was filled by nomination by the Governor from the membership of the same Protectorate Assembly. Thus when the first real steps toward independence were taken in Sierra Leone, the role of chiefs in the central government was firmly established as significant and indispensable.

Through the years the policy of the British Government on chieftaincy in Sierra Leone was characterized by a desire to reward chiefs with great power in the political structure of the country, no doubt in recognition of their proved loyalty. Perhaps also it was due to the confidence the British had in the institution of chieftaincy as the best framework for the superimposition of Western-style parliamentary democracy in the country. The British well knew that the chiefs, in protection of their own vested interests if for no other reasons, could always be counted on to give full support to the Government and to resist the forces of change in their communities.

In the decade after the implementation of the 1951 constitution, the chiefs played a very active part not only in the Legislative Council but also in the Executive Council. When the British, in keeping with their practice of giving African leaders supervisory authority similar to cabinet responsibility during the period of internal self-government, decided to appoint six Africans to hold such supervisory portfolios and become active members of the Executive Council, a chief was among the ministers appointed.[10]

But perhaps the most significant development of the chief's role in the story of Sierra Leone is his emergence as an active participant in party politics and the independence movement. Even though the chiefs enjoyed a special relationship with the British in a tacit alliance as "power brokers" in the country, they were clearly aware of their leadership responsibilities toward their people. The newly emerging educated elements in the Protectorate were drawn from the same chiefly elite class. The sons, brothers, relatives, and wards of chiefs were the individuals who had benefited from such educational opportunities as existed in the Protectorate. The missionary establishing a new school in any community had habitually drawn his first pupils from the chief's nominees, since the school in such a community would not have been possible in the first place without the chief's consent and support. When at last the British decided to set up a government school at Bo for Protectorate higher education, enrollment was restricted to sons and nominees of chiefs. This same policy was later followed when other government-sponsored schools were opened in the Protectorate. Even those Protectorate persons who ventured to send their sons to Freetown for higher education were drawn from the same group because only chiefs commanded the necessary economic strength to make such ventures possible.

The chiefs cleverly identified themselves with the political aspirations of their people for the independence of Sierra Leone. As they were identified with the educated and articulate sections of the Protectorate, they took the lead in demanding better political opportunities for the people. They were no doubt shrewdly aware of the inevitability of political change in Sierra Leone and concerned with ensuring their position as a class in the new scheme of things.

Thus when the Sierra Leone People's Party was formed—the party that was to take the country into independence—the chiefs were in the forefront of the leadership and greatly influenced its policy. As the organization dedicated to Protectorate interests, the S.L.P.P. unlike similar independence movements in other African countries, did not direct its main thrust against the British imperialists. It appeared to be directed more against the Colony and the Creoles. It was a question of which group of Sierra Leoneans was to take control of Sierra Leone's political affairs. In such a fight the chiefs considered themselves as well qualified as any other group to lead the Protectorate in rectifying the imbalance of their situation vis-à-vis the

Colony. One finds therefore that despite the record of the chiefs as oppressors of their people and collaborators with colonialism against the best interests of the people, they were able from the beginning of party politics in the country to participate actively and to identify themselves particularly with the leadership of the Sierra Leone People's Party, playing a most effective role in determining its tone and policies.

With this powerful influence of the chiefs on the entrenched elite of the S.L.P.P., it is hardly surprising that the party developed into a lackluster movement without any of the fiery revolutionary and nationalist enthusiasms of similar independence movements in other parts of Africa; nor is it surprising that the British Government appeared to give the S.L.P.P. its blessing and supported it at all times against any other party which of necessity had to be more nationalistic. The participation of the chiefs at this stage and at this level in Sierra Leone politics did much to moderate the tone of nationalism in the political development of the country.

When independence came in 1961, the chiefs emerged with tremendous political strength. This was discernible not only from the specific stipulations in their favor written into the Independence Constitution but also from the enormous influence they had proved themselves capable of wielding in the elections for ordinary members of Parliament from the various constituencies.

The Sierra Leone Independence Constitution of 1961 provided that members of Parliament should be drawn from two distinct categories of membership—Paramount Chief members representing each district of the Protectorate, and ordinary members representing constituencies from the whole country.[11] Since at the date of independence there were twelve districts in the Protectorate and forty-eight ordinary constituencies in the country, this provision meant that of the sixty members of the first Parliament after independence, twelve were Paramount Chiefs. Of the forty-eight ordinary constituencies, twelve were in the Colony and thirty-six in the Protectorate. There is no doubt that Paramount Chiefs have always exercised excessive influence in the election of ordinary members to Parliament from the Protectorate. Chiefs have been known to eject from their chiefdoms politicians whose views they do not care for. In the circumstances, opposition parties and politicians in the provinces have often been obliged to utilize tactics in their political campaigns that the Government has considered subversive and prejudicial to the maintenance of law and order. The chiefs, by completely identifying themselves with the Government of the day, have deprived the opposition in their districts of any other course of action but to confront the authority of the chiefs. In reacting to this challenge, the chief has had one of two choices: He can employ all the facilities at his disposal to thwart the opposition's efforts and mount a powerful defense of the Government's position, or he can remain silent in the face of such opposition attacks and thereby expose himself to charges by the Government of subversive activities. Not unnaturally, the chiefs have almost always chosen the first alternative. They know their destinies to be tied with those of the Government, and they also know it to be in their interest to support Government's policies completely. Thus, except in very rare instances, politicians who do not wish to incur the wrath of the local chief have been extremely loath to identify themselves with opposition groups.

Apart from ensuring for the chiefs a place in the legislative chamber, the 1961 Sierra Leone Independence Constitution was phrased in such a way as not to exclude chiefs from holding any ministerial portfolio including that of Prime Minister. All that the relevant section of the Constitution states on this point is that "Whenever the Governor-General has occasion to appoint a Prime Minister, he shall appoint a member of the House of Representatives who appears to him likely to command the support of the majority of the members of the House." [12] There is nothing in the Constitution to prevent chiefs from holding any other ministerial portfolio either. The relevant section only states that "appointments to the office of Minister, other than the office of Prime Minister, shall be made by the Governor-General, acting in accordance with the advice of the Prime Minister, from among the members of the House of Representatives." [13]

From these sections of the Constitution relating to the appointment of the Prime Minister and other ministers, it is quite clear that the only requirement is that such persons should be drawn from members of the House of Representatives. Since some chiefs were members of the House of Representatives, the only correct interpretation of these sections of the Sierra Leone Independence Constitution, in the absence of any enactment to the contrary, is that chiefs could quite properly be appointed to hold ministerial portfolios as indeed they have regularly been.

It is quite significant that when finally a breakdown occurred in the parliamentary process in March 1967, following general elections, and the military staged a *coup d'état,* it was largely due to a difference in interpretation of the exact role of chiefs within the parliamentary system. Brigadier David Lansanna, the Force Commander, explaining his reasons for the military takeover in his broadcast to the nation on March 22, 1967, stated *inter alia:*

> I saw him [the Governor-General] again on the day of the Chiefs' Elections and he informed me that despite the fact that neither Party had the majority and both were 32:32 equal, again I repeat 32:32, he proposed to make an appointment of a Prime Minister. I again informed him that I would not be able to contain any trouble which might arise if he acted unconstitutionally. Two hours after my interview with him, he decided to make an appointment when neither Party had a majority and Elections were still in progress.[14]

Thus it was clear to David Lansanna, and indeed many others in and out of Sierra Leone, that the Governor-General's conduct was precipitate and unconstitutional in appointing a Prime Minister before the conclusion of the elections of a whole category of Parliamentary membership. According to this argument, since chief members under the constitution enjoy equal voting rights in Parliament in such a closely run election, it was important for the Governor-General to await the returns of the elections of chiefs before deciding to invite the man who appeared to him "likely to command the support of the majority of the members of the House" to form a government. As it turned out, immediate events following his decision exposed the misjudgment of the Governor-General. When the elected chiefs declared their party allegiance, they overwhelmingly supported the S.L.P.P., giving the edge to Albert Margai over Siaka Stevens as the man in fact more likely to command the support of the members of the House.

The Dove-Edwin Commission of Inquiry into the conduct of the 1967 general elections in Sierra Leone agreed with the position taken by the Governor-General and stated in their report: "In not waiting for the results of the Paramount Chiefs' Elections before acting under his powers, the Governor-General, Sir Henry, was manifestly right." [15]

When the Commission undertakes to produce reasons to justify this position, one enters an area of doubtful logic and suspect law. The main position of the Dove-Edwin Commissioners was gingerly summed up as follows:

> We think that the Governor-General was right. The result of the Paramount Chiefs' Elections would not have helped him at all in coming to his decision. The most those Elections would reveal is that twelve Paramount Chiefs had been elected, each for his own District and nothing to do with the Parties. We have dealt with the meaning of "declared for the S.L.P.P." It simply does not mean a thing. In the Assembly, all Independents who wish to can cross over to the Party of their choice and it is then that the change of loyalties can be of any value.[16]

The Dove-Edwin Commissioners and the All People's Congress are no doubt of the view that the support of twelve paramount chiefs in the House of Representatives was of no importance and could well be ignored in an election in which, by their own evidence, the two major parties had been running neck and neck. When with reference to paramount chiefs' elections Mr. Dove-Edwin pronounces in his report, as though he were handing down profound oracular revelations from Mosaic heights: "The most those Elections would reveal is that twelve Paramount Chiefs had been elected, each for his own District and nothing to do with the Parties. We have dealt with the meaning of 'declared for the S.L.P.P.' It simply does not mean a thing," he was only stating what was equally true of the elections of all the members, ordinary as well as paramount chiefs. As a matter of fact, it is quite elementary that in British parliamentary electoral practice, the system from which the Sierra Leone parliamentary practice has been copied, parliamentary candidates contest for parliamentary seats as individuals and not as party members. They have always been quite free to support any party of their choice after Parliament convenes. It is, of course, well known to the constituents to which party a particular candidate belongs, or whether, as an independent, he does not belong to any. But the matter has been confirmed often enough in Britain that a member of Parliament, in spite of the party colors he might have adopted at election time, is in fact elected as an individual and quite free to change his allegiance in Parliament. This is a privilege enjoyed by all members, be they party members or independents. In the same way it seems quite clear to me that "declared for the S.L.P.P." in the case of the paramount chiefs cannot hold less meaning than in the case of ordinary members.

In their statement on the Report of the Dove-Edwin Commission, the National Reformation Council quite rightly rejected the Commission's view of the role of paramount chiefs in the parliamentary electoral process. In a forthright passage the National Reformation Council stated:

> The National Reformation Council does not agree with the conclusions reached by the Commission as regards the position of Paramount Chiefs in the House of Representatives. It is the view of the National Reformation Council that, since the House of Representatives consists of Ordinary as well as Paramount Chief Members, no House of Representatives can be legally constituted before elections of both categories of members have been duly concluded in accordance with Section 30 of the Constitution.[17]

The National Reformation Council thus underlined the importance of paramount chiefs within the parliamentary system of government in Sierra Leone. In their very next paragraph the National Reformation Council proceeded to reiterate the position which is quite clearly indicated in the Sierra Leone Independence Constitution of 1961:

> The paramount Chief members are therefore an integral and essential part of the House of Representatives.[18]

In expressing their views on the Dove-Edwin Commission's cavalier contention that "the result of the Paramount Chiefs' Elections would not have helped him at all in coming to his decision," [19] the National Reformation Council stated:

> Similarly, the Statement in paragraph 108 of the Report that the results of the Paramount Chief Members' Election would not have

helped the Governor-General at all in coming to his decision is incorrect, because he would not have been competent to appoint a Prime Minister if in fact no election was held for Paramount Chief Members.[20]

From this latest constitutional crisis in Sierra Leone, the position of paramount chiefs as a vital and integral part of the parliamentary system has emerged as an issue of the highest importance. Many who had previously dismissed their presence in the House of Representatives as a harmless anachronism and relic of the past will now have to give this question of the role of chiefs within the democratic processes in Sierra Leone more serious consideration. In commenting on the subject in the report of the Dove Edwin Commission of Inquiry into the conduct of the 1967 general elections in Sierra Leone, the Commission stated in paragraph 99:

> Twelve Paramount Chiefs were to be elected, one for each of the twelve Districts, primarily to represent their Districts. And again in paragraph 105: . . . We are satisfied that Paramount Chiefs represent their Districts and by and large support the Government.

Here again, the Dove-Edwin Commissioners have not said anything about elected Paramount Chiefs that is not also true of ordinary members. Ordinary members could well be said to have been elected to represent their constituencies, and, like Paramount Chiefs, they could also support the government if they chose. As was dramatized when the results of the Paramount Chiefs' elections were announced, Paramount Chiefs displayed a full awareness of their freedom to support not only the government but also the opposition and their right to declare themselves independent. One member, Paramount Chief Bai Kurr Kanasaky, III, of Tonkolili, declared openly for the A.P.C. in the same way ten others declared for the S.L.P.P. Paramount Chief Bai Koblo Pathbana, II, of Marampa Masimra, declared openly that he was an Independent at the time his election victory was announced.

No one can seriously deny that paramount chiefs have played as active a part as other members of Parliament in the legislative as well as in the executive aspects of government. Indeed, from the earliest beginnings of parliamentary government in Sierra Leone, their role has often been decisive. As was rightly observed by the National Reformation Council in their statement on the Dove-Edwin Commission's Report:

> There is in fact nothing in the Constitution to prevent the Governor-General appointing a Paramount Chief Member as Prime Minister if a Paramount Chief Member appears to the Governor-General a person likely to command majority support of the members of the House. Therefore, in appointing the Prime Minister before the election of the Paramount Chief Members, the Governor-General inadvertently deprived the Paramount Chief Members of their right to have one of their members elected as Prime Minister.[21]

As a matter of fact, ever since Africans began to exercise ministerial responsibilities in Sierra Leone, Paramount Chiefs have regularly been among those chosen for this privilege.

In the Sierra Leone Independence Constitution, the office of Paramount Chief is not only specifically mentioned but is included among the entrenched clauses requiring a special procedure for amendment.[22] Chieftaincy as such has not only been incorporated into the local administrative structure in the former Protectorate, but has been entrenched in the Constitution and Paramount Chiefs for good or for ill have been ensured a role of great significance in the legislative and executive processes of government in Sierra Leone.

It is my view that Paramount Chiefs should not be allowed to play the role the Constitution now permits them to play in the legislative and executive arms of government. While it is true that for the time being the cooperation of chiefs and the institution of chieftaincy may be necessary for administration in the provinces, there can be no justification for having Paramount Chiefs in the same chamber as ordinary members of Parliament. The historical effectiveness of chiefs in the evolution of government in Sierra Leone is beyond question. But as in the monarchies of Europe, such hereditary rulers must yield to the forces of change in an expanding democracy. These forces of change in the nature of things in Sierra Leone have to be activated by populist movements that will give the ordinary people an ever-increasing share in the government of the country. The natural conservatism that chiefs represent cannot be expected to force the pace for the evolutionary change that is vital for the progress and development of Sierra Leone.

There is no doubt that the emerging educated elements in the former Protectorate will not long leave unchallenged the hegemony of the chiefs and their class in the affairs of the Protectorate. With the spread of education this conflict will become more apparent. As long ago as 1950, the British colonial administration was fully aware of the growing discord between the chiefs and the new educated elements in that part of the country. The then acting governor, Mr. R. O. Romage, in a speech delivered to the Protectorate Assembly, identified old practices and customs with the chiefs and elders of the community and education and modern developments with the younger men of the community. He emphasized the necessity for both groups to work together in the interest of the country and made a strong plea that younger men should be given an adequate opportunity to take part in government.[23]

The most relevant role that the ordinary and younger members of the former Protectorate community can play in the system of parliamentary democracy in Sierra Leone is to participate vigorously in the election of the membership of the legislature. The chiefs for their part can well confine their activities to the executive arm of government through administration of their chiefdoms and leave to commoners the matter of central government legislation.

I believe that the place for Paramount Chiefs is in their chiefdoms where they can for the time being enjoy executive powers and preside over the affairs of their people. These executive powers, however, should be gradually curtailed in direct relationship to the educational advancement of the people. Power should be gradually transferred to a popularly elected local council whose members may be party supporters or nonparty civic leaders. Such a local council should be presided over by the chief who would draw his executive support and strength from the members of his council. Eventually, the chief's role should be that of a purely ceremonial and nonexecutive leader of his people. The nucleus of sound municipal government could well be established in this way and it should not be long before the office of chieftaincy is done away with completely and the political institutions of local government fully democratized.

If democracy is to have a real chance in Sierra Leone, it should be taken to its logical conclusion at all levels. It will not be enough for democratic principles to be used in certain cases and not in all.

It is certainly a negation of democracy for certain individuals within the body politic to have two votes when others have only one. A Constitution that allows elected Paramount Chief Members to sit in the same legislative chamber with Ordinary Members certainly makes it possible for the individuals who elect the Paramount Chief and the Ordinary Member of Parliament for the same district to enjoy the advantages of two votes.

Further, as long as chiefs hold positions of importance in the government and within the structure of the party in power, they could hardly be expected not to do their utmost to resist the forces of change within their communities and do everything possible to preserve the government in power as the only sensible and logical way to protect their own interests. For real progressive change to occur in Sierra Leone, particularly in the provinces, the chiefs should be made to refrain from participation in national politics and confine their activities to civic and administrative leadership in their communities. As long as chiefs identify themselves to any great extent with the party in power and with government policies, it will be inevitable that opposition to the policies of the central government will also be identifiable with opposition to the rule and authority of the chief. In such circumstances it will also be inevitable, as is currently the case in Sierra Leone, for chiefs to do all in their power to suppress all forms of opposition which they recognize as a threat to their personal positions.

If it is granted that the office of chieftaincy is vital for the time being for the administration of the provinces in a situation in which the majority of the people are not educated and are more adjusted to tribal and customary life, then for this reason the chief should continue to preside only over customary and traditional matters in the local provincial communities. With the spread of education in these areas, however, his position should become superfluous and his powers gradually handed over to a democratically elected municipal-type council.

In central government and political affairs, the chief should have no role, nor should he be allowed to take up any personal position in political and controversial affairs. These matters should be left in the hands of Ordinary Members of Parliament who are better qualified to take care of such public matters.

It may well be that a case can be made for the existence of a second legislative chamber where chiefs can meet with their colleagues from other areas to deliberate on matters of common interest pertaining to tribal and customary life. In such a chamber special interests, including religious and commercial groups, could also be represented. In this way, the office of chieftaincy would be protected from the strife of party political controversy and the chief restored to his historic role of being the guardian of his people and the protector of their interests for as long as they are in need of such guardianship and protection.

## NOTES

1. Christopher Fyfe, *History of Sierra Leone*, p. 2.
2. *Ibid.*
3. *Ibid.*, p. 3.
4. *Ibid.*, p. 19. The chiefs were King Tom and his subchiefs, Pa Bongee and Queen Yomacouba.
5. Kenneth Little, *The Mende of Sierra Leone* (Routledge & Kegan Paul, London: 1951), p. 90.
6. *Ibid.*, p. 91.
7. *Sierra Leone Protectorate Law Ordinance,* No. 16 of 1905, Sec. 15.
8. *Forced Labour Ordinance,* 1932.
9. *Cox Commission of Inquiry Report* (Freetown, 1956).
10. Bai Farama Tass, II, of Kambia in the Northern Province.
11. *Sierra Leone Independence Constitution 1961,* Ch. IV, Sec. 30 (1) (a) and (b).
12. *Ibid.*, Ch. V, Sec. 58 (2).
13. *Ibid.*, Ch. V, Sec. 58 (4).
14. *Report of the Dove-Edwin Commission on the 1967 General Elections,* Sec. 118 (Government Printer, S. L., 1967).
15. *Ibid.*, Sec. 104.
16. *Ibid.*, Sec. 108.
17. Statement of the National Reformation Council on the Dove-Edwin Commission's Report, Sec. 27 (S.L. Govt. Pub. 1967).
18. *Ibid.*, Sec. 28.
19. See note 16.
20. National Reformation Council, *op. cit.,* Sec. 32.
21. *Ibid.*, Sec. 34.
22. *Sierra Leone Independence Constitution 1961,* Sec. 44.
23. Seventh Protectorate Assembly Proceedings (S. L. Government, Freetown, 1950).

# CHAPTER 8

# Dilemmas of Independence

Nationalism as such did not provide the kind of impetus to the independence movement in Sierra Leone that was evident in many other African countries. The unique set of circumstances in Sierra Leone as reflected in the problems of the Colony-Protectorate issue, tribalism, and the role of chiefs did much to inhibit Sierra Leoneans from developing a nationalism like that which existed in most colonial situations and survived after independence to provide the inspiration and sense of direction likely to galvanize a people to dramatic national achievement.

The political parties that emerged in Sierra Leone in the post-World War II period had independence in sight and were clearly set on establishing themselves as the legitimate successors of the colonial administration. In every case, the leadership of these parties, both in the Colony and in the Protectorate, was drawn from the same elite class of chiefs and middle-class professionals that British colonial policies had created. More perhaps than in many other African countries, this elite leadership group in Sierra Leone was particularly anxious to take the expatriate colonial oligarchy's place as the "standard-setting group" in Nadel's phrase.[1]

Since the end of World War I, a middle class of professionals and civil servants had emerged, anxious to replace expatriates in the jobs and opportunities that only the colonial-government system could provide. This class of Sierra Leoneans, because of their relative educational and financial superiority, soon established themselves as the new leadership class. The brand of nationalism that developed, therefore, assumed a predominantly anticolonial flavor directed mainly at the removal of the colonial establishment which they recognized as the main obstacle. This colonial establishment included not only the civil service but also the expatriate commercial enterprises that collaborated with the British to implement an anti-African policy of employment and advancement into the higher grades of service.

The independence movement in Sierra Leone was thus a movement directed toward the removal of expatriates from positions of higher financial rewards and to their replacement by Africans equally qualified to hold such positions but who had been debarred by the implementation of a deliberate colonial policy. There were of course at the time vague and sometimes extreme declarations by politicians and political parties of intentions to utilize the natural resources of the country more in the interests of the people of Sierra Leone after independence. The glories and prosperity of an independent Sierra Leone were often painted in attractive colors to cheering audiences who had been led to believe that there was an inherent magic in the word "independence."

By and large, however, despite the feverish activities of the politicians, the country as a whole did not seem deeply involved in what was going on. The atmosphere did not exude that excitement and high expectancy one normally associates with such an historic impending event. This was largely because independence did not come as the result of a particularly difficult national struggle. No deep emotions had been aroused and no major battles fought, nor had there been any outpouring of national emotions in response to great rallying cries from national leaders. As a matter of fact, the vast majority of the people were totally oblivious of what was happening; they were not in any way personally and individually involved nor did they have strong sentiments for independence.

Those who knew and were deeply involved were the elite groups from both the Colony and the Protectorate. They were the people who had challenged the British colonial regime; and they were the people who were now about to benefit from the victory won. The victory, however bloodless, was indeed a victory. It was achieved through the quiet and unwritten alliance which the British had successfully established between themselves and the elite groups, both in the Colony through the professional classes and in the Protectorate through the chiefs.

In the Colony, wealth and education—which invariably existed together—had been the qualifications for social and political leadership. Adhering to British Victorian standards, the Creoles had recognized these attributes as the way to achievement and leadership. Those of their number who had enjoyed the advantages of education had been rewarded with the plums of society—moderately paid government jobs in the case of those who entered the civil service, and affluent careers for those who entered the professions. Through the years, the Creoles had known the social esteem accorded such persons by the British establishment. It was therefore the natural ambition of all Creoles that their children should receive the best education, thereby achieving wealth and eventual leadership in the community. Achievement of these British standards had enabled the Creole elite to establish this tacit alliance with the British, and had qualified them to be used as conscious and unconscious agents of British colonialism and for the diffusion of British culture not only in Sierra Leone but throughout West Africa.[2]

In the Protectorate, the focal point of leadership had always been with the chief, preserving wealth and influence within a given group. Colonialism had done nothing to change this state of affairs. Rather it had entrenched the chief in his position as the center of wealth and power in the community. Through the implementation of policies of native administration and indirect rule, the British had not only recognized indigenous and tribal institutions but had strengthened them. Thus was established a strong alliance between the chiefs and the Protectorate ruling classes on one side and the British on the other, for the successful implementation of colonialism and the expansion of British influence in the Protectorate.

When independence came, it amounted to a takeover by the Sierra Leone professional, educated, middle classes in alliance with the chiefly classes. The conservative character of the independence leadership dictated the policies pursued by the governing party after independence. The kind of change envisaged and planned for did not include ambitious programs for the introduction of social and economic equality, as one might have expected in a country with an average per capita income of less than seventy dollars[3] in which the elite groups easily have an average per capita income of at least fifteen hundred dollars.[4] The emphasis rather was put on the perpetuation of a free enterprise system which allowed, if it did not encourage, the well off and privileged to become richer, and the poor and underprivileged to struggle as best they could with little incentive to improve their condition.

It is true that one of the first things that an African-controlled government accomplished in Sierra Leone was the adoption of a much more ambitious educational program than had existed under colonialism. This new program included enormous aid to higher education, both on the university and the secondary school levels, making the all-important blessings of education more readily available to all sections of the community. Yet this educational program, ambitious though it is, has done little to bridge the educational gap existing between various sections of the community. Universal primary education, which has been considered to warrant the highest priority in many independent African countries, has not yet achieved that place of importance in Sierra Leone's educational planning. Other important needs of an education-conscious community, such as school buildings and teacher training, also remain quite low in the scale of priorities in national planning.

However, what gives cause for the greatest concern is the educational policy continued in Sierra Leone after independence. The colonial educational policy before independence had been completely patterned after the British system and geared to British cultural objectives. This was the case not only on the school levels but also on the higher education and university levels. Needless to say, whatever values there may be for the British in emphasizing classical education, these values have little meaning in an underdeveloped, basically agricultural country with over 80 percent illiteracy, whose population lives on a bare subsistence level. The British, with their penchant for exporting their own well-tried values as the only relevant ones in all circumstances, may be forgiven for equating these standards with "education" and "civilization." But it becomes a different matter when the policy planners in an independent Sierra Leone lamely and unimaginatively continue these same policies after independence. The general predilection for things British and the absence since independence of much original and nationalist thinking have made this sorry state of affairs possible. Maybe the Sierra Leone leaders had taken to heart too seriously their "preparation" for independence!

It has not been in the field of education alone that this lack of urgency and relevance in planning has been evident. In the areas of health and social services generally, unconcern has also been obvious. The Government in Sierra Leone since independence has not improved to any noticeable extent the public facilities available for medical services. During the days of colonialism, the British introduced free public health facilities through government hospitals and public health centers. But these services were nominal and barely met the minimal needs of the community. The Government after independence, on the whole, has continued these token services but has done little to improve and extend them. The attitude of the Sierra Leone Government toward the needs of the masses is best demonstrated by its policy with respect to the Social Welfare Department. Far from being the department to which Government is eager to give as much money and attention as possible, it is apportioned the lowest percentage of the national revenue. All this is not to say that a government faced with all the awesome and terrifying problems that colonialism had left unresolved would find it easy to cope with the important demands of independence at once. What is of significance and worth comment is the basis of priority applied in the new situation by the Sierra Leone Government. For example, cars with flags and chauffeurs, provided at public expense, became necessities for ministers, as did provision for ministers and senior civil servants of government quarters at subeconomic rents located generally in reserved sections of town. Much attention was paid to the trappings of office for the sake of status and prestige. The trend has been unmistakable. Members of the new elite are determined to establish themselves as a superior class and to widen rather than narrow the gap between themselves and the other groups in the country.

This process of polarization of class interests in Sierra Leone has been possible largely because the independence movement was led by a political group which, though it had links and contacts with the lower classes, did not emerge through highly organized party structures. Unlike what happened in some other African countries, in Sierra Leone the nationalist parties that spearheaded the independence movements were not highly organized with a central party hierarchy leading down to the lowest unit of the village committee. The machinery simply did not exist for dissemination of party policies to the village level nor for articulation of village opinion which might later be channeled to the party leadership. Except in the urban areas, where some party politics and policies are discussed, the leaders in

Sierra Leone have emerged almost naturally from the traditional system. The chiefs of course have done so hereditarily. The elected members of Parliament in areas away from the towns are often those who are themselves scions of chiefly families or who have the full support and sponsorship of chiefs. Invariably educational equipment has been considered a useful qualification for leadership. But since the educated often also belong to the same class, the leadership tends to emerge naturally. Even in the urban areas where there may be much political activity, the choice of the people often depends on personalities rather than on parties. The criterion, here again, is generally educational. Thus, the same privileged group of individuals has been able to emerge on its own personal merits without much aid from national political machines. These persons have not felt it necessary to identify themselves completely with the circumstances and problems of the grass-roots masses.

The conservative character of the leadership after independence has no doubt been greatly responsible for the fact that politics in Sierra Leone has so far failed to assume that quality of radicalism so evident in some other independent African countries. Sierra Leonean post-colonial political parties have never produced a Kwame Nkrumah, Sekou Toure, Leopold Senghor, or Julius Nyerere to articulate, if not always practice, those ideas of socialism, African or otherwise, which seem appropriate to the situation. This has certainly not been because the masses in Sierra Leone were less deprived by colonialism than were their counterparts in Ghana, Guinea, Senegal, and Tanzania where the nationalist political parties embraced socialism as the only desirable economic philosophy. It is simply that the mood in Sierra Leone has been different.

It was not only in the area of economic policies that politicians in Sierra Leone displayed a studied conservatism. The same attitude was in evidence in their relations with their former colonial overlords—the British. Independence in Sierra Leone was not celebrated as a great liberation from the yoke of imperialism or relief from an oppressive British rule. Rather, it was regarded as a somewhat peaceful transfer of power from generous and fraternal benefactors to well-trained and grateful friends. To many Sierra Leoneans, independence did not augur a dramatic or drastic break-away from the British and the past. There were those, particularly among the Creoles, to whom the idea of independence became acceptable only because it was understood that British connections would continue and that Sierra Leone was to remain in the British Commonwealth after independence. In fact, for some time after independence the most trusted advisers of important ministers, including the Prime Minister, were British officials.[5]

In such circumstances, the main thrust of policy and politics in Sierra Leone was to continue the system and the policies the British had bequeathed—a system rooted in British traditions and experiences and in keeping with British imperialist interests. The economic aspects of this system which Sierra Leonean politicians unfortunately embraced without much original thought were clearly a relic of British imperialism, conceived for the perpetuation of economic dependence on the mother country and geared more to British economic needs than to those of Sierra Leone.

At independence, Sierra Leone was a producer of primary products like palm kernels and piassava which were exported to Europe in the raw state and returned to Sierra Leone as manufactured goods in the form of soap, broom, etc. at considerable profit to the British. Distribution of the imported manufactured goods and marketing of the produce of the Sierra Leonean farmers was almost exclusively controlled by large European companies and their agents. The export and import trade in Sierra Leone, such as it was before independence, was solidly in non-Sierra Leonean hands. Just before independence, African firms handled only 2.9 percent of imports and only 1.4 percent of exports.[6] The situation was not much different in the case of companies registered and conducting business in Sierra Leone, less than a quarter of which were owned by Sierra Leoneans. What is more significant, of course, is that the average share capital of such Sierra Leonean-owned companies was about £12,000 as against an average share capital of £45,000 for foreign-owned companies. Moreover, in 1953 the average share capital of three foreign companies was £750,000 and six others in fact had share capitals worth over £1,000,000.[7] It is thus obvious that through this system Sierra Leonians were effectively excluded from participation in big business in the country and inevitably became victims of economic colonization.

By continuing this economic system after independence, the political leaders in Sierra Leone failed to decolonize the economy, and furthered a policy which was in itself, in my view, a negation of real independence. Let it be said that the British, in implementing these economic policies in Sierra Leone before independence, were not behaving differently from the way they habitually behaved in their other colonial possessions. This in fact was the classic colonial policy.[8] What was different so far as Sierra Leone was concerned was the failure of the political leaders after independence to appreciate the urgent need to discard such policies and the necessity to embrace only those economic policies directed toward economic decolonization.

In my view, the economic policies adopted by the Government after independence should have been centered around state planning. The Government should have assumed the responsibility of restricting the area of operation of foreign business interests and accepted increasingly the burden of state organization of the economy. If for no other reason, the capital necessary for the conduct of ambitious industrialization and rapid economic development could only flow from government. To allow free enterprise full rein and to support a capitalist economy was to ensure the total inability of Sierra Leoneans to achieve any appreciable measure of economic independence.

It is interesting to compare economic policy in Nigeria—a much larger country whose colonial experience, political and economic, is in many ways similar to that of Sierra Leone—of which the former Premier of Western Nigeria, Chief Obafemi Awolowo, stated in his recent book on Nigerian constitutional affairs:

> We must make up our minds, before it is too late to abandon our present slavish and unwholesome affection for a capitalist economy. Our own considered view is that no underdeveloped—now euphemistically called developing—country can make a success of any bold and radical development programme in an economy which is basically planless, and only partially planned.[9]

Another problem arising from the circumstances of the granting of independence to Sierra Leone has been that of the outlook and attitude of Sierra Leoneans as political leaders, civil servants, and citizens of an independent African country. During the decade or so immediately preceding independence, the British had gone to great lengths and taken infinite care to "prepare" and "train" Africans for independence. In the case of the civil service, this was to some extent understandable since such training was mainly technical and professional. But preparing political leaders for independence became another matter altogether.

Even the training given to civil servants has often been quite unsuitable for the postindependence needs of a small developing African country. Robert Gardiner, the leading Ghanaian economist and Executive Secretary of the United Nations Economic Commission for Africa, writing about the urgent problems of development confronting African countries has stated:

> The African school of today sticks to old notions of preparing civil servants. But modern civil servants must have a totally different approach. In colonial times their duty was to maintain security and an almost static, law-abiding society. Africa now has a fast-moving, rapidly expanding society in which problems must be solved at once.[10]

It was quite clear that the British were determined to hand over power only to a group of persons who had been properly indoctrinated in things British and most likely to keep Sierra Leone after independence within the British sphere of influence and dependent on the British economic system. There were those, in fact, who detected in the British eagerness to grant independence to Sierra Leone in 1961, and to hand power over to the pro-British conservative party of Milton Margai, a desire on the part of the West to establish a pro-Western regime next door to Guinea as a counterbalance in that part of Africa against the influence of the left-leaning Sekou Toure.[11]

The British had represented independence as the prerogative of the "prepared" man. Accordingly, preparation was conducted through a process of brainwashing the people into an involuntary acceptance of the attitudes and policies ordained for them. Through this procedure, the British hoped to ensure for themselves a position of influence and control long after nominal independence was achieved. The policy of economic dependence and subtle political involvement imposed by imperialist nations on former colonial territories is what Kwame Nkrumah has decried and described as "neocolonialism." [12]

In Sierra Leone, under the guidance and preparation of the British former colonial overlords, economic and foreign policies were adopted that were clearly in keeping with British interests, in the belief that such policies accorded with true democratic principles. In furtherance of them, diplomatic missions were set up in the United Kingdom and the United States of America but none in the Soviet Union, China, or any communist country. The young men who were trained for the Sierra Leone diplomatic service received such training in Britain and Australia. Not surprisingly, the highlight of their training was the inculcation of an unwholesome suspicion of communists and communism.

In the field of economics, free enterprise with no holds barred was accepted as the national economic policy. Incentives were even provided would-be investors to encourage them to participate in this extremely free enterprise economy. These incentives included "tax holidays" for up to five years in order to lure foreign capitalist companies to exploit the natural resources of the country. Milton Margai, encouraged by his British friends, proclaimed what he described as an "open-door Policy." Needless to say, foreign capitalist companies promptly availed themselves of these overgenerous terms and Sierra Leone has been suffering the loss of much-needed taxation revenue since.

Mercifully, many of these policies have subsequently been modified, particularly after the accession to power of the more progressive Albert Margai. Nevertheless, they operated long enough during the crucial years after independence to inflict irretrievable damage on the economic prospects of the country.

One of the main factors that led to the political breakdown in 1967 was the failure of the Government to solve the chronic economic problems inherited from the previous administration. It was inevitable that a small country like Sierra Leone should be confronted with grave economic problems at independence. There are many who seriously doubt whether such a small country, endowed with limited natural resources, could ever really be economically viable. All the more reason why, in my view, the policy of free enterprise was self-defeating and should have been rejected. State planning on a large scale, with limited free enterprise, should have been introduced. Certain sectors of economic development should have been exclusively reserved for government and quasi-government participation, and other sectors should have been made available for unrestricted foreign capitalist exploitation.

In the sphere of government, Sierra Leone inherited at independence a British-style constitution, based on Western democratic principles drawn especially from British political and constitutional experience. The constitution presumed a multiparty political system with a party or parties in government and a party or parties in opposition.

The circumstances of independence in most African colonial countries, however, produced one powerful nationalist independence movement built around a single political party. Even in those countries where there existed more than one party, several parties were willing to come together, forget their differencs, and join forces to overthrow the colonial yoke. In Sierra Leone, even though fierce nationalism as such did not play an important part in the independence movement, all the political parties in the country at the time of independence were willing to come together in a United National Front coalition, not only to agree on the terms of the Independence Constitution but to form the coalition all-party government that took Sierra Leone into independence. For all practical purposes, therefore, Sierra Leonean politicians came to realize at the most crucial stage in the country's history that the interests of the country could best be served through a united nationalist effort in every way analogous to a one-party situation.

The multiparty structure advocated as the democratic ideal in Western democracies is not suitable at this stage of development in a postcolonial African country. Many who would strongly argue against the one-party state forget that even in Western democracies the multiparty structure is not essential for the successful working of the democratic process. In the United Kingdom it is perfectly possible to elect a Parliament drawn from a single party or from no party at all. In the United States it is also technically possible to have an entire Congress drawn from one political party. Nowadays it is becoming increasingly difficult to draw clear-cut lines between party political positions or ideologies in these two bastions of Western democracy. Even if democracy as theoretically conceived with a multiparty system worked smoothly and satisfactorily in Western countries from whose political institutional experiences it emerged, this is no reason why it should necessarily be adopted in African postcolonial situations or regarded as the only satisfactory system of government.

The particular situation of postcolonial Africa, in my view, required the mobilization of the total human and natural resources of the nation. Independence itself was achieved in most cases as the result of the united effort of the whole nation behind a nationalist movement to overthrow colonialism. In many ways the national crisis that produced independence has continued after independence, and, as was the case at the beginning, a united effort is necessary to weld the nation together to cope with the continuing problems and challenges. Questions of ideology are irrelevant and superfluous since there can be no serious differences over national goals and objectives. The problems confronting an African postcolonial country at independence are always obvious. The leaders and the people need no ideologies to persuade them of their urgency and the necessity to find solutions. There can be no isms relevant to the building of schools, roads, and bridges. Whatever discussion may be necessary can well be conducted within the structure of the single-party organization. After all, Africans are quite familiar with processes of decision making within a group that permits a healthy and often vigorous and protracted discussion of the issues involved before a definite agreement emerges—a system that Gray-Cowan has called "consensus democracy." [13] The single party has the added advantage in an African context of involving the nation in mass participation in decision making. Since everyone is free to join the party, the party could in no way become the preserve of any particular class or interest group in the nation. Rather, it would involve everyone in the activities of the party and, through the party, with the tasks of government and the building of the young nation. The multiplication of political parties in a postcolonial African situation is a luxury which Africans can ill afford. As Madeira Keita has very aptly put it:

In the present historical situation in Africa, there is no need to multiply parties, nor to indulge in the luxury of a sterile and fratricidal opposition. Since we were agreed on the essentials and we're pursuing the same objectives, was there any reason to remain divided and split into parties that fought one another? [14]

One sometimes suspects that the strongest case that can be made for the multiparty structure in independent African countries is that it provides easy vehicles for subversion by interested foreign governments and interests, inasmuch as opposition parties have turned out in many instances to be a grouping of individuals anxious to procure the downfall of the legitimate government by the indiscriminate adoption of any tactics. Far from providing constructive criticisms or alternative policies to the government in power, opposition parties have tended to be as destructive and as disruptive as possible.

In the tribal situation in Africa, where so many tribes with different traditions and languages have found themselves within the same body politic, the problems of welding a new nation have much greater chance of solution in a state with a single party structure than in a multiparty structure where parties can be used to exaggerate, crystallize, and perpetuate tribal differences as has occurred in the celebrated case of Nigeria.

Perhaps the most important problem which has confronted tribal African countries after independence has been that of national unity. In order to cope successfully with the pressing challenges of independence, it is essential that the young nation should mobilize its efforts and potential rather than divide them. In a situation where the goals are clear and not seriously controversial a single party can well provide a satisfactory forum and the organ within which discussions and consensus formulation may be achieved.

For a one-party system in a West African postcolonial setting to succeed, it is essential that political power should be controlled at the top by a strong leader. Tribal Africa with the experiences of chieftaincy ought not to have much difficulty in accepting the supreme authority of such a leader who will express the will and personality of the nation. By such a procedure, the unity of the nation would be preserved within a framework of democracy.

No doubt due to its overwhelming advantages, most newly independent African nations today have adopted the one-party system of democracy. In Sierra Leone, however, perhaps because of the peculiar historical background, even though it was a one-party coalition government that ushered the nation into independence, there are those who would not accept the single-party system as in any sense democratic. Immediately preceding the achievement of independence, the All People's Congress party was formed and constituted the official opposition until the 1967 general elections. After a year of military rule, the A.P.C. assumed the reins of government in 1968. The A.P.C. has not produced a different set of goals or ideologies from those of the S.L.P.P., nor has it outlined any different methods of achieving those goals that both parties agree are desirable for Sierra Leone. The A.P.C., however, when in opposition charged the S.L.P.P. Government with corruption, inefficiency, and ineptitude and waged a tireless campaign to bring about its downfall. The S.L.P.P. Government even accused the leadership of the A.P.C. of complicity in a conspiracy to use violent methods through a *coup d'état* to remove the Government.

Perhaps the most significant feature of the existence of two parties in Sierra Leone has been the tribal cleavage that has manifested itself consistently in every general election. In the last general elections of 1967, for example, as has already been stated, the Mendes voted overwhelmingly for the S.L.P.P., and most of the other tribes voted solidly for the A.P.C. in the wake of a remarkable outburst of anti-Mende sentiment in the country. Thus, the multiparty structure has been instrumental in Sierra Leone in perpetuating tribalism. On the other hand, as Kwame Nkrumah was able to do in Ghana with his Convention People's Party, the one-party structure could well have been used in Sierra Leone to unite the people behind a national effort to achieve the real promise of independence. Unfortunately, it was not. When in 1965 Albert Margai, the then Prime Minister, mounted a national campaign to popularize the one-party idea, the opposition became fanatic and uncompromising. In fact, many date the beginning of his political decline to this period. His opponents employed all the usual arguments of Western critics against the single-party system. Chief among them was that the implementation of a one-party rule in Sierra Leone would lead to dictatorship and the eclipse of all forms of opposition. Once again, the contradictions and dilemmas of Sierra Leone's peculiar approach to independence were exposed.

When Sierra Leone achieved independence, there were many factors and problems in the country crying for urgent attention and solution. Leadership was passed on to an elite group that was not really anxious to change the order of society or to achieve social justice. Independence to this leadership group meant a change of the identity of the ruling class—from the British to the African elite that had been "prepared" for independence. Democracy as a political principle was accepted both for the working of the constitution and as an organizational way of life. The implications of democracy, in an African context, unfortunately escaped the leaders. The real role of the chiefs as a leadership class within the democratic process was a contradiction that was glossed over. The long-standing and unnecessary Colony-Protectorate problems were shelved. The logic of nationalism was not pressed to its conclusion. In fact the rhetoric of change essential for real nationalist independence was never heard. What took place was the expression of a genuine desire for progress along the lines the British friends of the leaders had mapped out for them.

The road the British mapped out at independence inevitably led to continued economic dependence and economic colonization. The democracy that was to be emulated and the institutions supporting the system temporarily collapsed in the wake of stalemated elections. All the old antagonisms of the Colony-Protectorate cleavage surfaced once again. At this stage, all the ingredients were present for a breakdown of an unworkable system, and the first experiment with democracy in Sierra Leone was doomed. In spite of the lip service they paid to democracy, the people of Sierra Leone proved themselves to be essentially tribal and to possess many characteristics in common with people who faced similar problems in other parts of Africa.

It was inevitable that an independence conceived essentially as a continuation of the system that prevailed before independence would lead to serious problems and create dilemmas. For independence to have a real chance of success in an African postcolonial situation, a radical approach should be adopted in the formulation of new policies—an approach that, unfortunately, was not taken in Sierra Leone. Now that constitutionality has been restored, the optimistic can still hope for another experiment with democracy in Sierra Leone. However, the same problems persist and it is difficult to see how democracy in Sierra Leone can succeed without radical changes in attitudes and in the constitution itself.

## NOTES

1. S. F. Nadel, *The Concept of Social Elites,* International Social Science Bulletin, Vol. III (1956).

2. Fourah Bay College was founded by the Church Missionary Society (England) in 1827 at Freetown. Students have been awarded Durham University degrees there since 1876.

3. *Selected Economic Data for Less Developed Countries,* U.S. Agency for International Development, May, 1963.

4. These groups would include lawyers, doctors, dentists, executive engineers, chiefs, businessmen, and senior civil servants whose starting salary is at least 1,000 Leones per annum, the equivalent of 1,400 dollars.

5. The Prime Minister at independence was Sir Milton Margai, and he retained as his secretary, at independence and for some time afterwards, Mr. Martin Page, a British colonial official.

6. N. A. Cox-George, *African Participation in Commerce,* p. 8.

7. *Ibid.,* pp. 14–15.

8. L. Gray Cowan, *The Dilemmas of African Independence* (Walker & Co., New York), Chap. 2, p. 30.

9. Obafemi Awolowo, *Thoughts on Nigerian Constitution* (Oxford University Press), p. 161.

10. Robert K. A. Gardiner, *The New York Times,* January 26, 1968, p. 59.

11. Guinea achieved independence in 1958 under the leadership of Sekou Toure who had led his people to defiantly vote "No" in the French referendum that year—the only French Colonial territory to do so.

12. Kwame Nkrumah, *Neocolonialism,* 1964.

13. Cowan, *op. cit.,* p. 12.

14. Madeira Keita, an official of the Union Sudanaise, the governing party of Mali, in an article published in 1960. *Ibid.,* p. 8.

# CHAPTER 9

# The End of an Experiment

It was perhaps inevitable that the experiment in democracy in an independent Sierra Leone, saddled with such fundamental contradictions, had little chance of real success. The problems seemed endemic and insurmountable. With pressures increasing every passing month, the general political situation appeared to defy solution.

The experience in Sierra Leone has clearly demonstrated that it is not enough for an independent country to adopt a well-written independence constitution. Democracy and good government are not necessarily ensured by "entrenched clauses" safeguarding minority rights in such a constitution. For democracy as a system of government to survive in an African postcolonial situation, there must be much more. As the Nigerian leader Obafemi Awolowo has very wisely observed:

> Democracy is more a way of life than a creature of constitution. To change the metaphor, it is to a large extent an affair of the heart. All that the constitution can do is to create an atmosphere and construct a machinery which are respectively congenial to and helpful in the pursuit of democracy. The actual and conscientious pursuit of this ideal depends on the right type of leadership, and on a vigilant, enlightened and irrepressible public. The latter we are beginning to have; but the former is yet to arrive.[1]

From the standpoint of the constitution and the system of government existing in Sierra Leone after independence, democratic institutions were undoubtedly in evidence. What was grievously lacking was the atmosphere in which democracy could thrive. In a constitutional situation in which political parties habitually reflect tribal sentiments, democracy becomes endangered when tribal antagonisms assume serious proportions. Unfortunately, this has been the case in Sierra Leone since independence. In a situation in which chiefs, as representatives of the ruling classes, participate in the legislative process in the same chamber and with the same rights as ordinary members, who represent ordinary citizens, it becomes questionable whether the chiefs and their class do not exercise an unwarranted influence over the affairs of the ordinary people. Above all, in a situation in which the opposition assumes a belligerence almost amounting to a threat to the preservation of law and order and the right of the government to govern, it becomes doubtful whether democracy is not a system of weakness, and completely unsuitable for the orderly progress of that particular society.

As has previously been stated, when Milton Margai's government led Sierra Leone into independence, it was in an atmosphere of great cordiality with his British friends whom he often jokingly referred to as his "brothers." The policies embarked upon after independence fully reflected a desire on the part of the Sierra Leone Government to continue uninterrupted this blissful relationship. Milton Margai's well-publicized "Open Door" economic policies constituted striking examples of his willingness to continue following the planning and economic policies British colonialism had left behind.

For example, the Sierra Leone Government during the first two years of independence, and while Milton Margai was still Prime Minister, contracted many long-term foreign loans carrying high interest rates. The Government also, during those first few years, participated as part owners with foreign companies in quite a few dubious development projects which seem to have brought profits to the foreign companies and loss to the Sierra Leone Government.[2] To many objective observers at the time, it was quite clear that Sierra Leone would find it extremely difficult if not impossible to meet the annual commitments involved in servicing these loans and at the same time balance the nation's fast-expanding budget. Even in those areas of economic planning in which the Government appeared to have invested prudently, time was very much of the essence, as the projects needed years before discernible advantages could accrue to the country.

Meanwhile, the economic burdens of independence were becoming more pressing as diplomatic missions sprang up abroad, and the difficulties of meeting the rising expectations of the people became more severe. With every year of independence, the public expenditure became greater and the expectations of the people more demanding. They now became impatient of economic deprivation which, apparently, they had been quite willing to endure under British colonialism. Since the rate of economic growth failed to rise any higher than 2½ percent, the gap between government expenditure and income continued to widen.

When Milton Margai died on April 28, 1964, the fiscal and economic problems of Sierra Leone were severe. The Government was just then beginning to realize that unless something urgent and dramatic were done, the economic situation of the country would continue to decline and soon become desperate. This was the national economic legacy Albert Margai inherited when he became Prime Minister of Sierra Leone on April 29, 1964.

Albert Margai's ascendancy was greeted in Sierra Leone with overwhelming and almost universal approval. Those who had been aware of the deterioration of the economic situation heaved a sigh of relief in the belief that a sure and steady hand had at last taken hold of the reins of government. Even his political detractors held their fire for a while, impressed by the wind of national optimism which was blowing through the nation. But this mood did not last long. Within eighteen short months of his assumption of office, Albert Margai's administration had run into trouble. The storm of opposition, particularly from the Colony area, blew with unabated intensity and was never really calmed until the *coup d'état* that followed the general elections of March 1967. In appraising the circumstances of the military takeover in Sierra Leone, it is useful to consider the role played by the central figure in the whole drama, the Prime Minister, Albert Margai.

Despite the public display of enthusiasm and support that greeted his assumption of office, there were many who held deep-seated personal grudges against him and some who hated him passionately. During the nearly twenty years of his public life, Albert Margai had violated many political taboos and ruffled many conservative spirits on his way to supreme office. These antagonisms all had to do with the significance of the personal role he had played in the political history of Sierra Leone. It was Albert Margai who, immediately after returning home in 1948 from his legal studies in England, had dared to challenge the Colony Creoles' dominance of Sierra Leone politics. He then had rallied Protectorate political consciousness around the banners of the all-powerful Sierra Leone People's Party which soon seized control of organized politics in the country and kept it for many years. It was also Albert Margai who had led the avant-garde of the young educated elements in the Protectorate in the nineteen-fifties in their challenge to the traditional leadership of chiefs and elders in the Protectorate political hierarchy. He was the S.L.P.P. politician and leader whose name was anathema to the colonial authorities in Sierra Leone, who in 1957 had done all in their power to prevent him from wresting the leadership of the party from his clever and acquiescent older brother, Milton.

Albert Margai's entire political career had been characterized by impatience for change and restlessness of spirit which endeared him to nationalists and marked him for special hostility by conservatives and reactionaries. It was this radicalism which had led him in 1957 to lead an unsuccessful revolt against Milton Margai's traditional and conservative leadership of the S.L.P.P. It was this radicalism which had also led him into the political wilderness in 1958 and to the formation of the People's National Party in that year. When in 1964 he had at last arrived at the Prime Ministership, all the chickens, so to speak, "came home to roost."

Confronted with the grave economic problems he had inherited, Albert Margai, with characteristic vigor, took measures which he considered most likely to improve the situation. He sent his Minister of Finance abroad to negotiate further aid and loan programs. He negotiated successfully, for example, Sierra Leone's participation for the first time in the United States' P.L. 480 Agricultural Aid Program. Internally he put a new urgency and emphasis on agriculture. He was fully aware of the uncertainties of the diamond and mineral industries which contribute so much to the nation's revenue, and was most anxious to develop alternative sources of national income. He organized the farmers into cooperatives to enable them to market their produce more satisfactorily. To alleviate the unemployment problem, the Government sponsored large-scale agricultural development projects in various parts of the country to absorb large numbers of unskilled workers. He embarked on a policy of encouraging small industries in which the Government had substantial part-holdings.

Internationally, he was eager to translate Sierra Leone's avowed nonalignment policy into reality. Albert Margai strengthened diplomatic relations with the Soviet Union and did what the former Prime Minister had refused to do—he sent an envoy to Moscow. He considered it important that Sierra Leone's voice should no longer be shrill and vacillating in international forums, but should become articulate and effective. He participated personally and dramatically in British Commonwealth Prime Ministers' Conferences and Organization of African Unity meetings. He thus achieved for Sierra Leone, internationally, a new prestige and effectiveness. But the cost of these international posturings was high and aggravated somewhat the financial problems of the country. Albert Margai, however, has always been a man of unbounded optimism. He somehow felt confident of his ability to pull the country through the financial crisis. He appeared to believe that there was a relationship between international adventurism and the capacity to attract financial and trade assistance from the international community.

Politically, on taking office as Prime Minister and thus becoming leader of the S.L.P.P., Albert Margai realized that something urgently needed to be done to organize the party whose machinery had been allowed to rust during the preceding years. He toured the country extensively and exerted great efforts to make the people aware of what the Government was doing and rally them to the tasks of nation building.

Albert Margai's interest and involvement in international affairs, sharpened no doubt by his visits abroad, had made him deeply aware of the limitations of Western-style democratic institutions in the postcolonial situation. His actual experiences as Prime Minister apparently reinforced these convictions and he became increasingly disenchanted with the multiparty brand of democracy the British had bequeathed Sierra Leone. Above all, his nationalist spirits had been no doubt outraged by the divisiveness, sectionalism, and tribalism which he believed the two-party system not only made possible but encouraged. He therefore expressed grave concern that the future of democracy in Sierra Leone and the existence of the country as a unitary state would be seriously endangered if the multiparty system were continued.

He believed that the political salvation of the country lay in the early adoption of a one-party system of government which he had observed in successful operation in many African countries. With characteristic vigor and enthusiasm, Albert Margai proceeded to recommend the one-party idea to the people of Sierra Leone. Some believe that he might have had a more satisfactory response if he had employed better tactics, knowing the basically conservative temperament of Sierra Leoneans. The immediate reaction of the articulate and educated elements of the country, particularly in the Colony area, was extremely hostile and uncompromising. The continued advocacy of the one-party state only hardened the opposition against him. The opposition saw the one-party system as a prelude to dictatorship and the efforts of Albert Margai to recommend it to the country as clear evidence of his overweening personal ambition. Even though after some six months of public discussion of this issue Albert Margai withdrew his proposals, the damage to his credit had been done and from then on his every move was watched with the utmost suspicion.

Albert Margai's internal political difficulties at this time did not emanate exclusively from the opposition parties. There was a small but powerful radical group within his own party, made up predominantly of young lawyers and intellectuals who loudly proclaimed their disenchantment with the policies the party leadership was following. They were eager for the adoption of more radical policies and felt that Sierra Leone politics and government were outmoded and not in step with the new African nationalist thinking evident in other parts of Africa. This group had come to identify Albert Margai personally with what they considered to be the mismanagement of the country's economy and its policies generally. While they scrupulously refrained from identifying their position with that of the A.P.C., they nonetheless expressed their opposition to Albert Margai as the leader of the S.L.P.P. and made no secret of their desire for a change of leadership.

There was also a group of older members of the S.L.P.P. who had never forgiven Albert Margai for the role he had played in opposition to Milton Margai's conservative leadership of the S.L.P.P. Many of these, especially Mendes, traced the current disorganization in the ranks of the S.L.P.P. to Albert Margai's defection in 1958 and the formation of the P.N.P. These individuals, including many who were Ministers in Albert Margai's government, felt estranged from him and fretted and grumbled that he appeared to rely more on his young former associates of his P.N.P. days for guidance and advice than on the old clique of cronies who had exercised much power during the tenure of office of Milton Margai. In this particular view, these disgruntled S.L.P.P. old-guard leaders found sympathy among many other sections of the community, including the opposition. According to this argument, Albert Margai, had never really lost his antipathy to the old conservative wing of the S.L.P.P. nor had he lost his personal P.N.P. ambitions. They hinted that he had returned to the S.L.P.P. coalition government at independence only as part of a carefully planned strategy to install, as soon as convenient afterwards, all his former P.N.P. political friends in positions of power and influence; thus that group would eventually impose their P.N.P. policies on the nation.

Margai's detractors therefore reserved special hatred for all those personal associates of his who had worked with him during his P.N.P. days, and who were now in positions of prominence in the country's affairs. They saw in the existence of this group a national threat and the working of a conspiracy to impose Albert Margai's dictatorial rule on the country. As it happened, most of these friends of the Prime Minister were not in active politics but in positions of high public office. So, while Albert Margai was in a position to use their services and their advice, many of them were not in a position to help him within the scope of party politics. He was therefore in a position of political weakness, not only so far as the opposition was concerned but also within the S.L.P.P. whose old guard felt alienated from him. To compound his difficulties further, he had inherited a cabinet from Milton Margai whose members predominantly belonged to the S.L.P.P. old guard and included a few of the radical young S.L.P.P. politicians who felt disenchantment toward Albert Margai's personal leadership.

In spite of Margai's efforts to improve the economic health of the country, in the short run the financial situation continued to decline. Triggered no doubt by this development, his opponents began to point accusing fingers at his well-known personal fortune. Conveniently overlooking the fact that he had been Prime Minister for less than two years and that he had been known to be a man of substantial private means long before assuming the Prime Ministership, his opponents accused his government of corruption and clearly implied that he and his friends had been personally involved in "bleeding the nation white" financially. Successful criminal libel actions were brought against the editor of a leading local newspaper for allegations such as these, nevertheless, they had been repeated so often and so persuasively that many people believed them.

Albert Margai's fortunes as a political leader and as a man were clearly at a low point at the end of 1966. The opposition of the A.P.C. and the Colony Creoles had reached hysterical proportions. The military was becoming restless and the rumors of *coup d'état* were persistent.

Sierra Leone politics has always been responsive to political events in other parts of West Africa, and particularly in other former British colonial territories such as Ghana and Nigeria. In January 1966, West Africa and the world had been shocked by the news of the violent overthrow of the legitimate government of Nigeria as a result of a military *coup d'état*. In February 1966, the hero of African nationalism himself, Kwame Nkrumah, was also overthrown as a result of a *coup d'état*. With political tensions mounting in Sierra Leone, the army was being pressed by opposition and subversive elements to emulate what the disaffected considered good examples set elsewhere in West Africa and overthrow Albert Margai's government by military action.

The Force Commander, Brigadier Lansanna, however, was completely loyal to Albert Margai, his tribesman. When it became apparent that such military intervention could not occur with David Lansanna's connivance, the subversive political elements contented themselves with conspiring with younger and junior officers. Thus, during the year preceding the military takeover, there were many instances of serious insubordination and disloyalty among junior military officers. In fact, only three weeks before the final breakdown occurred, the Government unearthed an alleged plot to murder Albert Margai and other leading public servants connected with his government. In the alleged conspiracy, civilian politicians as well as young military officers were accused. At the time of the eventual military takeover, some of the military officers were under arrest awaiting a military trial. This development of an assassination conspiracy caused near panic in Freetown. Since the Government had in its possession what it considered to be conclusive evidence of the complicity of certain individuals, many of these persons and their friends were naturally nervous as to what the Margai government would do in retaliation. After the initial general consternation, however, there was public relief that bloodshed had been averted.

This was the atmosphere of bitterness and fear, of political desperation and conspiracies, of strife and tensions that prevailed in Sierra Leone, particularly in the Colony area, when the Prime Minister announced the dissolution of Parliament and fixed a date exactly a month later for general elections.

Although it was well known that elections were due at any time, many had speculated that in view of the unfavorable political climate, Albert Margai would take advantage of the discovery of the plot against his life to suspend the Constitution, declare a state of emergency, and assume dictatorial powers. Under the Sierra Leone Independence Constitution, it would have been perfectly permissible for him to do this, provided he did not suspend Parliament for more than a year.[3]

The Independence Constitution provides that general elections be held for the assembly of a new Parliament at least once every five years. In keeping with British constitutional practice which Sierra Leone had adopted, it was of course within the discretion of the Prime Minister to advise the Governor-General acting for the Queen as nominal Head of State of Sierra Leone to dissolve Parliament at any time convenient to the Prime Minister during that five-year term. The opportunity to use this option to his own advantage has always been one of the great political trumps available to the Prime Minister under this system. The S.L.P.P. government had unfortunately waited until the last possible moment to exercise what by then had ceased to be an option. The situation, therefore, in early 1967, was one in which everyone knew that if the constitutional provisions were to be respected, and in the absence of a state of emergency, general elections would have to be held within the next few months since the last ones had been held in May 1962.

Albert Margai chose, however, not to declare a state of emergency. He rejected the advice of those of his friends who strenuously counseled him against calling elections. He was deeply committed to legality and constitutionality and was particularly anxious not to do anything which might smack of irregularity and political cowardice. He had based his public career above everything else on boldness and courage and saw no reason why he should deviate at that stage from the policy of public conduct he had set himself. The elections were therefore held as originally scheduled on March 17, for ordinary members and March 21, 1967 for chief members.

The election campaign was conducted in an atmosphere charged with tensions and unbridled tribal group animosities, particularly in the Colony area. There was little evidence, however, of violence in the Colony. The electorate in this area seemed to have made up its mind and was indeed surprised and grateful that the elections were being held at all. In certain parts of the provinces, notably in the Kono district, there were some disturbances reflecting the multitribal composition of the population.

The Governor-General, fully aware of the seriousness of the political impasse that was developing in the country when most of the results of the election of ordinary members had become known, invited the leaders of the two parties—Albert Margai for the S.L.P.P. and Siaka Stevens for the A.P.C.—for consultations on March 20, 1967. He asked them to consider seriously the possibility of forming a coalition government, because, as he told them, he had concluded from his observation of the trend of the election returns that the people had voted tribally. It must have been clear to the Governor-General that if any one party had formed a government, a situation of serious tribal bitterness and confrontation might have ensued not only in Parliament, but throughout the country. This might well have led to the frustration and breakdown of the democratic process.

Unfortunately, Siaka Stevens promptly rejected the Governor-General's proposal and insisted that he was in a position to form a government. Albert Margai, confident that the results of the elections of chiefs on the next day, March 21, would give him an over-all majority in any event, preferred to wait until Wednesday, the 22nd, before committing himself, though he carefully refrained from rejecting the Governor-General's offer out of hand. Unfortunately, also, the Governor-General did not insist on a coalition government as he was constitutionally in a position to do but capitulated to pressures from persons who had no special political standing but were citizens of the Western area,[4] biased against Albert Margai and determined to remove him from office.

On March 21, 1967, before the elections for the chiefs had been held, the Governor-General appointed Siaka Stevens Prime Minister. There are strong and conflicting views on both sides as to the wisdom and constitutionality of the Governor-General's conduct.

The Dove-Edwin Commission of Inquiry [5] into the conduct of the 1967 general elections in Sierra Leone supported the Governor-General's actions and stated quite unequivocally that he was right.[6] The Statement of the National Reformation Council on the Dove-Edwin Commission Report took issue with the findings of the Commission on this matter, stating categorically that the Governor-General's conduct was "untimely" and had given rise to "an increasing tension throughout the country." [7] The National Reformation Council even went further and rebuked the Chairman of the Commission, Mr. Justice G. F. Dove-Edwin, a Creole, for complicity in the pressuring of the Governor-General when, in its statement, it accused him in the following terms of what amounted to professional misconduct:

> The National Reformation Council was both shocked and surprised to learn during the course of the Inquiry, that Mr. Justice Dove-Edwin, the Chairman of the Commission, had been one of the people who had been present at the State House at the material time.[8]
>
> *        *        *        *        *
>
> It is the view of the National Reformation Council that the Chairman of the Commission, having been confronted with this evidence, should have tendered his resignation.[9]

At the time, however, Brigadier Lansanna, the Force Commander, was clearly of the view that the Governor-General's conduct was unwise and unconstitutional. When Lansanna learned of the appointment of Siaka Stevens, in spite of his advice to the Governor-General to wait until the results of all the elections including those for chiefs were known, he surrounded the State House with his troops and kept the Governor-General, the new Prime Minister, and those who had accompanied him for the swearing-in under house arrest at the State House. Brigadier Lansanna announced to the nation that evening that he had no intention of assuming supreme power, but was only anxious to prevent the Governor-General from violating the Constitution. It was his view, the Force Commander stated, that by his appointment of a new Prime Minister in those circumstances, the Governor-General had acted *ultra vires* the Constitution. Next day, March 22, in further explanation of his action, the Brigadier stated in a broadcast to the nation:

On Saturday, the 18th March, after the elections of the Ordinary Members were over and the country was waiting for the elections of the 12 Paramount Chiefs representing the Districts, the state of the Political Parties was All People's Congress (A.P.C.) 32, Sierra Leone People's Party (S.L.P.P.) 32 and Independents 2.

It appeared that the results of the elections had reflected not political opinions but tribal differences. This meant that neither the Sierra Leone People's Party nor the All People's Congress had a majority because, as I have pointed out, the number of seats being 78, 32 on either side was less than the required majority of at least 40. Tension was building up in the country and as Chief of State Security I interviewed the Governor-General on the 19th and 20th of March, 1967, that is to say two days and one day before the other Elections were held, and informed him that a dangerous situation would be created if he made any appointment when neither party had a majority and the Elections had still not been concluded.

I saw him again on the day of the Chiefs' Elections and he informed me that despite the fact that neither party had the majority and both were 32:32 equal, again I repeat 32:32, he proposed to make an appointment of a Prime Minister. I again informed him that I would not be able to contain any trouble which might arise if he decided to make an appointment when neither Party had a majority and Elections were still in progress.

I want to make it clear that the Army—and I say this after consultation with my senior officers—does not, I repeat does not intend to impose a Military Government on the people of Sierra Leone. This country has a record for constitutional Government.[10]

And so constitutionality was suspended in Sierra Leone. What David Lansanna, the Force Commander, began and expected to be temporary, soon developed into something more menacing and not so temporary. To demonstrate his avowed unwillingness to impose a military regime on Sierra Leone, Lansanna promptly invited all the newly elected members of Parliament to meet with him on the evening of March 23 to choose a new Prime Minister or to decide on any other course of action for the resolution of the political crisis. This meeting, however, was never held. A group of ambitious junior officers revolted against David Lansanna, arrested and detained him, seized power and imposed a military regime.

In his speech to the nation on March 23, 1967, after the military *coup d'état,* Major Charles Blake spoke in familiar but unconvincing tones when he stated *inter alia:*

> Fellow citizens, I want to make this quite clear that we the senior officers do not intend to impose a Military Government on the people of this our beloved country. . . . I want to remind you, my dear people, that we are soldiers and politics is not our ambition. We will hand over to the politicians as soon as the situation becomes favourable. The National Reformation Council will do all in its power to bring about a civilian government in the shortest possible time.[11]

Only a year afterwards, Sierra Leone witnessed another military coup. It was a revolt of young noncommissioned officers against the senior officers of the ruling junta. This time, however, the promise of a speedy return to civilian rule was kept. One week after the coup, on April 26, 1968, Siaka Stevens, the leader of the All People's Congress, was installed as Prime Minister. But in the experience of these easy military takeovers, a terrible message has reached the people. The great unresolved problem confronting everyone is that of the obvious insecurity of any government in a situation in which any group of persons armed with guns can so easily overthrow one regime and set up another. This is indeed a crucial problem afflicting all of postcolonial Africa where serious attempts at operating a democratic system have been made.

How long the new civilian regime in Sierra Leone will last unmolested is a matter for conjecture. The first experiment with a democratic system of government in postcolonial Sierra Leone came to a sudden and dramatic end after less than six years of uneasy existence. It seems unfortunately clear, however, that unless the problems attending the democratic processes in Sierra Leone already outlined are resolved, the future prospects for democracy in Sierra Leone are very tenuous indeed.

## NOTES

1. Obafemi Awolowo, *Thoughts on Nigerian Constitution* (Oxford University Press, 1966), p. 157.

2. The National Construction Company established in 1959 was a case in point.

3. Suspension of S. L. Consti. Decl. of state of emergency for not more than one year. S. L. Indep. Consti. 1961, section 25 (4) of ch. 2.

4. Statement of the National Reformation Council on Report of the Dove-Edwin Commission of Inquiry, pars. 36, 37, and 40 (Sierra Leone Government Publ. 1967).

5. The Dove-Edwin Commission of Inquiry was appointed by the National Reformation Council on May 23, 1967, "To enquire into the conduct of the last General Elections held on the 17th and 21st days of March 1967. . . ." Govt. Notice No. 647, *Sierra Leone Gazette,* May 23, 1967.

6. Dove-Edwin Commission Report, par. 136 (2) (S. L. Govt., 1967).

7. National Reformation Council, *op. cit.,* par. 42.

8. *Ibid.,* par. 37.

9. *Ibid.,* par. 39.

10. Dove-Edwin Commission, *op. cit.,* par. 118.

11. National Reformation Council, *op. cit.,* par. 49.

# CHAPTER 10

# The Role of the Military in a Developing African Nation

An unfortunate feature of postcolonial Africa has been the remarkable regularity with which country after country has been overtaken by military coups. The pattern has often been the same—a group of armed men, sometimes acting for the whole army, at other times acting in rebellion against the army itself, overthrows the legally constituted government, seizes power, and installs a regime of its own choice. The governments such groups install have sometimes been drawn exclusively from their own ranks, and at other times have included civilians whose independence of action is generally suspect.

That military intervention should now constitute such a threat in independent Africa is a most regrettable development, a development that poses the greatest threat to the future of democracy as a system in that continent. As long as such intervention threats exist, there can be no guarantee that the will of the people as expressed through the ballot-box can have much chance of long enduring. There will always be the danger of some dissatisfied elements inspiring a military intervention when for one reason or another they wish to remove the legally elected government.

This situation has raised further serious questions as to the wisdom of imposing on an African country, with grave tribal and development problems, a system of government so closely copied from Western-style democracy and institutions of government. As long as the colonial power is in control with overwhelming force at its command, democratic institutions can be imposed without danger of armed intervention from any section of the populace. But when at the coming of independence the superior colonial military capability is withdrawn, the fate of democratic institutions is left entirely in the hands of the people themselves. At this stage the absence in a tribal society of that necessary ingredient of democracy that enables the individual in the state to accord to elected individuals the right to govern, irrespective of their tribal or regional background, becomes crucial. In country after country, a victory at the polls has not necessarily ensured for the victorious party uninterrupted tenure of office.

There is no doubt that this situation has developed in many newly independent African countries because of the absence of any real sense of national unity. Independence found many tribes and groups within these countries in fundamental opposition. No sense of nationhood existed. The uniting force was the tribe. Unfortunately the necessary healing processes after independence had not much advanced before the weaknesses became intolerable and found expression in military coups.

It is important to recognize that in most cases the military coups have not installed any better or more progressive regimes than those they have replaced. In the case of Sierra Leone, for example, the National Reformation Council, in spite of its promises and bombast, turned out to be much more corrupt than the civilian regime it replaced with so much fanfare and simulated reforming zeal. The National Reformation Council did not produce any dramatic solutions to the grave development and financial problems that had been plaguing the country. Nor did the National Reformation Council unite the people or give them a greater sense of nationhood.

The reasons for the failure of the military to provide better government in postcolonial Africa are quite clear. During the period of colonialism when Africans were being educated, the policy was to create an elite class capable of limited participation in the learned professions and of filling certain lower and middle levels of the civil service. The army was at the bottom of vocational choices available to a young man. The wages paid were barely at subsistence levels and attractive only to illiterates. As a matter of fact, there was a time in Sierra Leone when the only means open to the Government to fill the ranks of the army was by compulsory recruitment. For many years only illiterates joined the army in Sierra Leone. Even when, just before independence, the Government embarked on a deliberate policy of enlisting educated young men for officer training, they were seldom able to attract those who were in a position to enter the more fashionable and better-paid professions and the civil service. Consequently, the quality of men who joined the army was distinctly lower than that of the university graduates in the professions, in politics, and in the higher grades of the civilian government service. It was therefore not surprising that when the military junta seized power in Sierra Leone, it was not able to approximate to any extent the civilian parties' capacity to govern.

A further noteworthy point is the fact that in Africa the military as such do not belong to an identifiable class as is the case in certain Latin American and European countries. To begin with, the size of the army is generally very small in relation to the rest of the population. Also, the military are drawn from the same tribal groups from which the politicians and leaders are drawn. In Sierra Leone it is impossible to describe the military as representing any class. They do not represent even the least educated elements in the country as there are many more representatives of this class outside the army.

The only distinctive factor about the army in postcolonial Sierra Leone has been that, apart from the Civil Service, the army represents the only organized and disciplined group in the country. At independence, the political parties were neither strong nor well enough organized to fill the vacuum created by the withdrawal of British power. With tribalism in full cry, sufficient national cohesion did not exist to enable the people to submit to the necessary disciplines for nation building. The Civil Service, thanks to the training of the British, had the necessary expertise and discipline to successfully conduct the responsibilities of administration. The army on the other hand, with little more to do than drink excessively all day, had the necessary organization and discipline to take advantage of the weaknesses of the body politic and to pose an eternal threat to the workings of the democratic process.

The role of the military in a developing country requires the most serious consideration. It is no longer possible to ignore the threat of the army to peaceful constitutional government. All talk of democracy and the democratic processes becomes meaningless in the face of such a reality.

In colonial days, the army's role was primarily to preserve internal security and to protect the country's frontiers from encroachment.[1] Thus its duties were primarily confined to police actions as the British were always in a position to directly undertake whatever massive military intervention was considered necessary. It was the advent of independence that caused the Sierra Leone Government to expand the military capability of the army, enabling its officers and men to become aware of their potential for decisive intervention in the politics of the country. The mistaken notion had been accepted that there was some connection between the possession of a strong army and the prestige of an independent country.

I believe that small countries like Sierra Leone should face up squarely to the realities and limits of power in the middle of the twentieth century. Such countries should acknowledge that for protection against outside aggression of any massive nature, they cannot rely on their own military resources. The answer should lie in the contracting of mutual defence treaties and arrangements with more powerful countries. Preference naturally should be given to such alliances within the African continent. In the absence, however, of such alliances within Africa, realistic recognition should be given to the necessity of contracting such alliances with more powerful countries outside Africa. These are days of quick transportation and easy communication. A small country in Africa can easily sustain such a relationship with a country in Europe or in America as indeed many small African French-speaking countries have done with France.[2]

With security from outside and major internal aggression assured through mutual defense alliances with stronger powers, it should no longer be necessary for small African countries like Sierra Leone to maintain large armies. A small army of highly trained men properly disciplined to supplement the effectiveness of the police should be adequate for the police and security needs of a country like Sierra Leone.

Even after a great reduction in the size of the army, it will still be necessary to consider the proper role the army should play within the democratic system of government. It is my view that the army should be represented by its commander in the civil government and that he should be given a place in the cabinet as Minister of Defense. Thus the army will share in the decision-making processes of government and will have a direct stake in the security and stability of the nation. In such a role, the army would lose the independence from the civil administrative system it now enjoys and will not be in a position to consider itself outside the main structures of government. Since its commander would thus become a member of the civil government, the Prime Minister as head of that government would also assume the responsibilities of the Supreme Commander-in-Chief of the army.

The government should thereafter embark on a policy of educating the officers and men of the army about the functions of government and explaining to them the policies and aims of the government. In this way the members of the armed forces would come to play an integral part in the affairs of the country and closely identify themselves with its fortunes within a democratic system of government. It ought to be possible in such circumstances to remove the prevalent threat of army intervention since with such close identification of the army with the civilian administration, the army would in a sense be prejudicing its own interests by a military takeover.

There will still be the question of how to prevent junior officers and noncommissioned officers from rebelling against their superior officers in such close collaboration with the civilian government and thereby overthrowing the government itself. The answer should lie in the high quality of discipline which it would be important to maintain among all ranks in the army. The answer should also lie in the seriousness with which the program of educating the officers and men of the army on the policies and plans of the government is conducted.

With the army brought into the closest contact with the civilian government and the army accorded an integral role of influence in the workings of government, it ought to be possible to remove much of the threat of military intervention which now hangs over the governments of small African countries like Sierra Leone.

## NOTES

1. The army in British West Africa during colonial days was known as the West African Frontier Force with separate regiments in each of the four British West African territories (Nigeria, Gold Coast, Sierra Leone, Gambia). Its function as the protector of the country's territorial integrity was thus emphasized in the use of the word "Frontier" in the name.

2. France intervened in Gabon in the early sixties, to prevent a popular revolution; the United Kingdom intervened in 1964 to quell army mutinies in Tanzania, Kenya, and Uganda. Belgium has persistently intervened in the Congo's internal affairs since the Congo's independence in 1960.

# CHAPTER 11

# A Prognosis for Future Stability

The military junta that seized control in Sierra Leone on March 23, 1967, in spite of promises for the early restoration of civilian rule, clung tenaciously to power until it was violently overthrown by a counter coup staged by noncommissioned officers on April 18, 1968. Following the counter coup, a civilian government was installed by the appointment of Siaka Stevens, the All People's Congress leader, as Prime Minister, on April 26, 1968.

The return to civilian government in itself is not likely to produce lasting solutions to the vexing problems, already outlined, that afflict Sierra Leone. Serious thought will have to be given to these urgent problems to ensure the continued existence of democracy and democratic processes. It ought to be clear to anyone that unless some new procedures are adopted there can be no guarantee that another constitutional breakdown will not occur nor that the army will not again intervene and seize power.

In my view, there is clearly a place for democracy in any future constitutional arrangements in Sierra Leone. The background and experience of the people demand and justify this. Democracy as a system of government was not introduced into the country from outside. Long before the days of colonialism, the indigenous institutions of tribal life, including chieftaincy, had been based on ideas—albeit limited—of democracy. Chiefs have been always elected by their people and continue in office only by the consent of the people. Even the elders that surround and advise the chief owe their positions to the goodwill and tacit consent of the people of the chiefdom. Persons in authority, including the chief, can always be removed if the people so desire. In the Colony area before the colonial period, the people, through their background in slavery and the early beginnings of the Colony settlement, had been well accustomed to government according to democratic principles. Through the tribal headmen of the Liberated Africans and the civic leaders of the Freetown settlers, Sierra Leoneans had known the satisfaction of being led and governed by individuals of their own choice.

The role of chiefs in any new constitutional arrangements, in my view, should be much different from what it has been hitherto. The institution of chieftaincy should be modernized to meet the needs of an evolving society. Although principles of democracy are respected and applied in the choice of a chief and in his relationship with his people, the present system is far from satisfactory. As a first step toward the modernization of this institution, the office should be open for election to any member of the community, and not confined, as at present, to a few hereditary families, rotating the succession. The process already started by the central government to limit the jurisdiction of the chief's court should be accelerated. The chief's functions should be limited to the purely symbolic and ceremonial. His executive, administrative, and whatever may be left of his judicial powers should be exercised only through an advisory council. Such a council of elders should be elected by the people and made responsible to them. The chief's authority would thus be reduced to ceremonial and leadership duties very similar to those exercised by a mayor in a modern municipality. Such modernization will have the effect of reducing the chief from the position of an authoritarian ruler to a leader of his people within the local context.

Paramount Chiefs should be debarred from any participation in party politics since such involvement will inevitably embroil them in controversy. Their duties and influence should be strictly confined to their particular chiefdoms. If the chief's dignity and prestige as the undisputed leader of all the people of his chiefdom is to be preserved, he should be made to rise above the divisiveness of party politics. In such a situation, opposition as well as government politicians will enjoy equal treatment in their political activities in his chiefdom. He would not then be obliged either to defend or protect the government's position as he is now understandably often accused of doing since he would have no vested interest in the survival of any particular party in power. The constitution should not permit membership of Paramount Chiefs in the same legislative chamber with ordinary elected members. If chiefs should participate at all in national central government affairs, such participation should take place in another chamber.

If democracy is to have any meaning in Sierra Leone, there should be strict consistency in its application. If the people are to be governed by a central government popularly elected, the authority of government at all levels should be derived from such a central government. The hereditary system to which chiefs now owe their positions cannot be justified by the application of democratic principles. The chief's local functions should be only those allowed him by the central government, through a Minister of Internal Affairs.

Chieftaincy in its present form and operation appears to be quite inimical to progress and modernization and more suitable for a state of affairs which no longer exists. Undoubtedly, chieftaincy has played a useful role in the development of the country, particularly during the days of general illiteracy and extreme underdevelopment. Those were the days when tribal institutional life was all the people knew, and the need for community cohesion around the chief was very great. But with progress, education, and modernization sweeping through the country, the chief's traditional role is rapidly becoming superfluous and obsolete. The young men and women returning home from the universities and institutions of higher education in Sierra Leone and from all over the world can hardly be expected to feel the same need for chiefly traditional leadership. The democracy that will make sense to them will have to be consistent at all levels and fully responsive to modernization.

Sierra Leone should have a Republican constitution. It is a mockery of independence for an African state, previously colonial, to have the Queen of England as Head of State. To me the question of continuing in the British Commonwealth is not important as long as the obligations of this relationship continue to be vague and the policies governing it flexible and uncertain. But Sierra Leone should have a president as Head of State as soon as possible.

The President of Sierra Leone should hold executive powers and be elected by the whole country for a single fixed term of six years.

No President should be allowed to succeed himself. The President's duties should combine those now exercisable under the Independence Constitution by the Governor-General and the Prime Minister.

It is important that the President's position be strong and that he be able to enjoy complete control for a number of years. With its experience and appreciation of chieftaincy, the nation should be able to relate to such a strong executive and to understand the need for such centralized authority. The President in his person would symbolize the unity and personality of the nation to a people well familiar with traditional chiefly leadership. The possession of executive authority would remove the President from the level of party personality conflicts and spare him many of the indignities of strife and compromises.

There should be a Cabinet of Ministers appointed by the President at the beginning of his term of office and removable at the President's pleasure. Such ministers should be appointed from among persons inside and outside Parliament, provided the President does not appoint more than a third of his Cabinet from outside Parliament. Cabinet Ministers appointed from outside Parliament should have the right to speak and answer questions in Parliament, but not to vote. This system would have the advantage of employing elected representatives of the people as Ministers, as well as utilizing the services of eminently capable citizens who might not enter public life through the crucible of Parliamentary elections.

Parliament should comprise two chambers—the House of Legislature and the Senate. Ordinary members elected from the various constituencies all through the country should sit in the House of Legislature. Paramount Chiefs and traditional leaders representing districts, as well as representatives of special economic, cultural, and religious interests, should sit in the Senate. All legislation relating to finance, national income, and expenditure should be passed in the House of Legislature where only duly elected representatives of the people would sit, plus the nonvoting Cabinet Ministers who have been appointed from outside Parliament. The House of Legislature should also have full responsibility for all matters of foreign policy, development, and defense, including external and internal security.

The Senate should confine its activities to deliberations respecting noncontroversial matters on a nonparty basis. Decisions of the Senate would then have the effect of recommendations to the House of

Legislature for further action. The Senate would thus be useful as a forum for the discussion of tribal customary matters, providing an opportunity for Paramount Chiefs and tribal elders to exchange views on matters of mutual interest. The Senate should also provide a forum for discussion of special commercial problems as well as cultural and religious ones. Such discussions ought to be particularly valuable at a time when the cultural identity of the nation is in process of discovery and development.

In my view, any future constitutional arrangement in Sierra Leone should provide for the existence of only one political party. The necessity for national unity at this stage in the nation's history should rule out the proliferation of political parties. Political parties should be tolerated only when they are likely to facilitate the democratic process, but not when they are more likely to be used to obstruct and subvert that process. Given the realities of tribalism in Sierra Leone, the multiparty system provides an agreeable vehicle for the perpetuation of tribalist cleavages and sectionalism. The one-party system would provide a rallying organization for the development of nationalism—an organization in which everyone interested in politics or public affairs would feel free to participate. Under a one-party state, candidates for the ordinary seats in Parliament, that is, for the House of Legislature, would be expected to belong to the national party. Membership in the party would be open to everyone and as many members of the party as so desire could stand for Parliament in any constituency. Thus, when the people chose their representatives they would be making a choice among individuals and not among parties. Inevitably, out of the dynamics of the one-party system, a strong caucus of party activists would emerge within the party.

The party's policies should be completely devoted to the nation's interest as a whole and not to the interests of any particular group of persons. Its main task should be the establishment of a coherent structure with direct links from the party hierarchy at the capital to the lowest level at the village. Through committees and regular party meetings, a continuous colloquium and dialogue should be conducted, channeling the views from the grass roots level to the top, and making known at the village level the decisions of the leaders. In this way, party policy would keep contact with popular opinion at all levels and real democracy would be ensured. The leader of the party, through this system, would inevitably be elected President, as the system would lend itself to much emphasis on the personality and influence of a strong individual who would combine in his person the leadership of the government and the party. Thus, through the system of a one-party state, the will of all the people of Sierra Leone would be represented. Further, and highly important, there would be mass participation in decision making and involvement of all the people through a sense of personal responsibility in government.

As has already been stated, for Sierra Leone to have much of an economic future, the Government should embark on policies of extensive long-range planning. The sectors of the economy for Government control and participation and those for private foreign participation should be clearly defined. Those sectors of the economy relating to mineral resources and key products of mass consumption should be controlled by the Government. Of those sectors of the economy not publicly owned by Government and left to the area of private enterprise, a substantially greater share should be encouraged to remain in local and African hands rather than in the hands of foreign companies. There should be a definite and unrelenting trend away from all forms of foreign economic interest in the country and toward control and ownership by the Sierra Leone Government and toward private ownership by Sierra Leoneans.

To the extent that the Government can afford to do so, it should accept the responsibility of supplying the capital and technical personnel necessary for Sierra Leonean participation in the business life of the country. The policy developed by Albert Margai of encouraging heavy concentration in agriculture should be accelerated.

Large-scale industrialization, as far as resources permit, should also have a high priority in Government planning. This will, of course, require additional capital, which will have to come from loans or grants from foreign governments or from private external sources willing to collaborate with the Government on specific projects. To cope with the problems of ambitious modernization, the Government will have to adopt policies of educational planning for the training of technicians and entrepreneurs vital for the advancement of industrialization.

In the realm of foreign policy, Sierra Leone would be well-advised to adopt a policy of positive nonalignment. It should be important for Sierra Leone not to be the satellite of any major power nor to belong to any political grouping outside the Organization of

African Unity. Sierra Leone has nothing to gain from an involvement in the East-West cold war confrontation. On the contrary, Sierra Leone will have much to gain in terms of aid, trade, and cultural exchange if the country preserves excellent relations with the United States of America, the Union of the Soviet Socialist Republics, China, France, and the United Kingdom. The major policy position of Sierra Leone internationally should be that those policies alone will be followed which will protect the national integrity of the state while preserving friendly relations with all nations. This policy, however, should not inhibit Sierra Leone from taking bold and independent positions on matters of grave international morality. The country's external posture at all times should reflect the earnest striving of its people to approximate to the highest standards of social justice and equality. However, the overriding consideration in foreign affairs should be to keep Sierra Leone solidly in tune with African policy in those matters in which a policy has been adopted by the Organization of African Unity.

A small African country like Sierra Leone should be acutely aware of its inseparable links with other African countries, particularly neighboring ones. The economic viability and prosperity of the country will largely depend on the economic cooperation that can be achieved with other African countries.

I am strongly of the view that Sierra Leone should begin to be involved in an active economic cooperation with neighboring countries, beginning with the establishment of a customs union which would eventually develop into a full-fledged regional common market. From such economic cooperation with neighbors, Sierra Leone should seriously consider entering into a complete political union with her neighbors. This collaboration and eventual union of Sierra Leone with neighboring African states should be the main plank of the future one-party state.

Sierra Leone, with Liberia and Guinea, can easily form a federal union if the leaders seriously address themselves to this task. The federation at its early stages should be loosely tied, with much autonomy left to the constituent states. The main spheres of government that the federal union would assume would be in the areas of foreign policy, economic policy, and defence. If the relationship proves worthwhile and successful, the federal government can enlarge its sphere of responsibility. Detailed constitutional proposals should be worked out providing for a federation Parliament, with equal representation from each state.

A Federal Union of these three countries would be highly desirable and workable. Many of the major tribes of the countries are not confined to any particular one of them. The people belong to the same tribes and have always mixed freely. Many of the citizens of the three countries speak common languages. Even though in these countries many languages are spoken, yet the members of the leadership class in all three countries speak either English or French and sometimes both. There are many examples in other countries where more than one official language is used.[1]

Sierra Leone's first experience with democracy after independence failed. After a year of military rule, another effort is being made. There is every reason to believe that in the years that lie ahead, if the necessary lessons are learned from the experiences and mistakes of the past, Sierra Leone could well have a great future full of exciting possibilities for the well-being of the individual within the state. Much, of course, will depend on the extent to which new and satisfactory solutions are found for old problems. It is my belief and my hope that such a future can best be achieved within a union of West African States, including the neighboring states of Guinea and Liberia.

## NOTE

1. Countries in which more than one official language is used include Canada: two; Belgium: two; Switzerland: two; Philippines: three.

# Index